SPAN

GW01452594

BAKING COOKBOOK

Along with 350 recipes is a comprehensive guide to traditional and modern Spanish baking techniques, recipes, and flavors

By

Loyal Pepin

TABLE OF CONTENT

INTRODUCTION

Welcome to the rich world of Spanish baking, where a delightful variety of pastries, bread, and sweets is created by the seamless fusion of centuries-old traditions with contemporary methods. With this cookbook, we welcome you to embark on a gastronomic exploration of the various areas of Spain, each boasting a distinct culinary legacy and riches.

Spanish baking embodies the diverse history, culture, and topography of the nation, ranging from the sun-kissed beaches of Andalusia to the untamed highlands of Catalonia. Spanish food is a mix of flavours and ingredients that is both thrilling and comfortable, with influences from the Moors, Romans, and other civilizations.

This book contains a variety of classic recipes handed down through the ages, along with contemporary adaptations that highlight the inventiveness of today's bakers. Everything from well-known classics like flan and churros to lesser-known treats like ensaimadas and tortas de aceite can be found to satiate every savoury and sweet craving.

This handbook contains recipes for both experienced and inexperienced bakers who want to learn more about the world of Spanish pastries. Thus, gather your aprons, fire up the oven, and get set to go on a delectable journey through the captivating tastes of Spanish baking.

Cheers to your success!

CHAPTER - 1

TOOLS FOR BAKING BREAD

To get the desired results, baking bread requires a combination of ingredients, methods, and equipment. Here is a detailed list of all the tools that are typically used for baking bread:

Mixing and Preparing Dough:

1. Getting Ready for Dough: Large dishes for kneading dough and combining ingredients are used for mixing.

2. Hand or stand mixers: Electric mixers with dough hooks for effective dough kneading.

3. Bench scraper: Used for scraping off sticky dough, cleaning work surfaces, and cutting dough.

4. Dough Whisk or Wooden Spoon: Use a wooden spoon or dough whisk to stir dough by hand before kneading it.

5. Measuring Cups and Spoons: When baking bread, precise ingredient measurement is essential.

Kneading and Shaping:

1. Dough Scraper/Bench Knife: During kneading, a dough scraper or bench knife can be used to divide the dough and scrape it off surfaces.

2. Rolling Pin: A rolling pin is helpful for shaping and flattening the dough, particularly for flatbread recipes.

3. Proofing Baskets (Bannetons): These provide the final structure and shape of the bread by shaping and proofing the dough.

4. Couche Cloth or Linen Towels: Linen towels or couch cloth are used to support the dough during its last rise.

Baking:

1. Baking Stone or Baking Steel: When baking, use baking stone or baking steel for crisp crusts and equal heat distribution. It can be made to resemble a brick oven by preheating it in the oven.

2. Baking Sheet or Tray: Use a baking sheet or tray to bake bread, rolls, or flatbreads.

3. Dutch Oven or Bread Cloche: A Dutch oven, often known as a bread cloche, produces a steamy baking atmosphere that promotes oven spring and crust formation.

4. Lame or Razor Blade: To score the bread dough before baking so that it expands appropriately while baking, use a lame or razor blade.

5. Thermometer: Assures that the bread is baked to the proper internal temperature, which for most bread is usually between 190 and 210°C (375 and 410°F).

6. Gloves or oven mitts: To properly handle hot bakeware.

7. Cooling rack: This rack allows air to circulate around it to prevent the cooked bread from becoming soggy.

Optional but Useful:

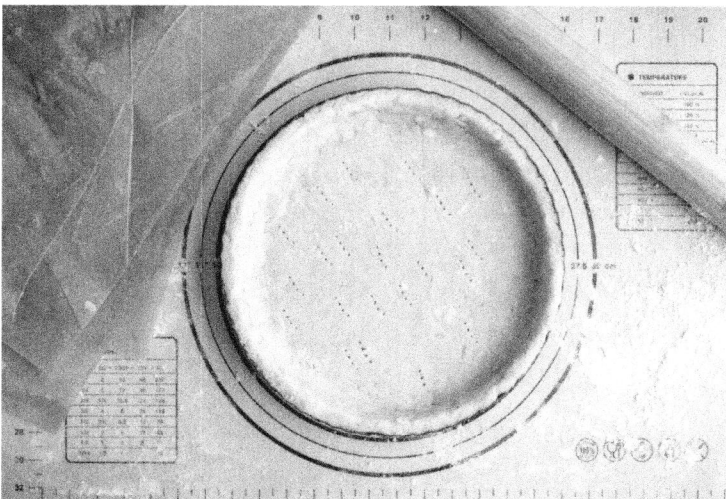

1. Parchment paper or silicone baking mats: They make cleanup simpler and prevent sticking.

2. Spray bottle: To encourage crust growth while baking, apply steam to the oven.

3. Bread Scoring Tool: A tool made expressly to score dough, offering increased control and accuracy.

4. Bread Machine: Mixing, kneading, rising, and baking are all done in one unit by bread machines, which are ideal for people who prefer a more automated procedure.

Preservation and Storage:

1. Bread Box or Bread Bag: Use a bread box or bread bag to store bread and prolong its freshness.

2. Plastic Bread Bags or Wrapping: Individual loaves or pieces can be frozen or stored using plastic bread bags or wrapping.

Having this equipment at your disposal can ensure consistent outcomes with every batch of bread and make the baking process more fun and efficient.

What information is necessary before beginning to bake bread?

To ensure success, there are a few essential things you should know before you begin baking bread. Here's a thorough guide:

Ingredients:

- Flour: All-purpose or bread flour is frequently utilized. The greater protein content of bread flour aids in the development of gluten.
- Yeast: Two standard options are quick or active dry yeast. While active dry yeast must first be activated in warm water before use, instant yeast can be added to the flour straight away.
- Water: To activate the yeast and combine it with flour, use lukewarm water.
- Salt: Crucial for flavour and for regulating the activity of yeast.
- Sugar/Honey: Adds taste and nourishment for the yeast. can aid with browning as well.

Equipment:

- Bowls for mixing: These are used to combine and let the dough rise.

- We are measuring spoons and cups For precise measurement of ingredients.
- Kitchen scale: Beneficial for exact quantities, particularly when measuring flour.
- Stand mixer or hand mixer: Kneading can be done by hand or with a stand mixer fitted with a dough hook attachment.
- Using a Dutch oven or baking pan depends on the kind of bread you're creating.
- Make sure your oven is at the right temperature with an oven thermometer.

Techniques:

- Kneading: Work the dough to include gluten. It gives the bread flexibility and structure.
- Depending on the recipe, this can be done one or more times.
- Shaping: Before the last rise, the dough is shaped into the desired shape.
- Scoring is the process of scoring the surface of the dough with a razor or sharp knife before baking. This enables the bread to rise in the oven as it should.
- Baking is the last stage in which the bread is baked. Typically, this entails setting the oven's temperature and preheating it.

Recipes and Ratios:

- If you're new to baking bread, mainly stick to a reliable recipe.
- Take note of the proportions of salt and yeast, as well as the flour-to-water ratios.

Environment:

- Bread-making can be impacted by temperature and humidity. Fermentation proceeds more quickly in warmer temperatures and more slowly in cooler ones.

Patience and Practice:

- Baking bread is both an art and a science. If you fail on your initial try, don't give up.
- Your talents will improve with practice. Take note of the specifics and gain knowledge with every batch.

Troubleshooting:

- Be ready to solve typical problems such as over- or under-proofing, dense bread, etc.
- Knowing what went wrong will enable you to improve your approach the following time.

Safety:

- Consistently adhere to fundamental food safety protocols, including hand washing and maintaining a tidy workspace.
- Exercise caution when handling hot appliances and machinery.

Taking note of these specifics will ensure that you're ready to start making delectable bread at home. Recall that experience makes perfect, so feel free to try new things and pick up new skills along the road.

CHAPTER - 2
SPANISH BAKING FOR BEGINNERS (EASY RECIPES TO START WITH)

Churros with Hot Chocolate

Churros Ingredients:

- 1 cup water
- 2 tablespoons sugar
- 2 tablespoons vegetable oil
- 1 cup all-purpose flour
- 1/4 teaspoon salt
- Oil for frying

Hot Chocolate Ingredients:

- 2 cups milk
- 100g dark chocolate, chopped
- 2 tablespoons sugar (optional)
- 1 teaspoon vanilla extract

Instructions:

1. Bring the water, sugar, and vegetable oil to a boil in a saucepan.

2. Turn off the fire and mix in the flour and salt to form a dough.
3. Preheat the oil in a big skillet or deep fryer to 180°C (350°F).
4. Spoon the dough into a piping bag and insert a star tip into it.
5. Using scissors, cut 6-inch dough strips as you pipe them into the heated oil. Fry for 2 to 3 minutes on each side or until golden brown.
6. Take out the oil and place it on paper towels to drain the churros.
7. In a separate saucepan, bring the milk to a gentle simmer. Remove the heat and stir in the vanilla essence, chopped chocolate, and sugar (if using). Mix the mixture until it becomes smooth and the chocolate has melted.
8. Present the hot chocolate to dip alongside the churros.

Apple Turnovers

Ingredients:

- 2 apples, peeled, cored, and diced
- 1/4 cup sugar
- 1 teaspoon cinnamon
- 1 tablespoon lemon juice
- 1 package puff pastry sheets, thawed

- 1 egg, beaten
- Powdered sugar for dusting (optional)

Instructions:

1. Set the oven temperature to 200°C or 400°F. Use parchment paper to line a baking sheet.
2. Put the diced apples, sugar, cinnamon, and lemon juice in a bowl.
3. Cut the puff pastry sheets into squares after rolling them out.
4. Fill the middle of each square with a spoonful of the apple mixture.
5. To form a triangle, fold the crust over the filling and press the corners together to seal.
6. Transfer the turnovers to the prepared baking sheet after brushing them with beaten eggs.
7. Bake until golden brown, 15 to 20 minutes.
8. If desired, let cool somewhat before sprinkling with powdered sugar.

Spanish Cupcakes

Ingredients:

- 2 eggs
- 1/2 cup sugar
- 1/2 cup vegetable oil
- 1/2 cup milk
- 1 teaspoon vanilla extract
- 1 1/2 cups all-purpose flour
- 1 1/2 teaspoons baking powder
- Zest of 1 lemon

Instructions:

1. Set the oven temperature to 180°C or 350°F. Use paper liners to line a muffin tray.
2. Beat the eggs and sugar together in a bowl until light and frothy.
3. Add the milk, vanilla essence, and vegetable oil gradually while thoroughly combining.
4. Gently mix in the flour and baking powder until just incorporated after sifting them in.
5. Add the lemon zest and stir.
6. Spoon the batter into each muffin cup to a depth of two-thirds.

7. Let the cake bake for 15 to 20 minutes or until a toothpick inserted into the middle comes out clean.
8. After the cupcakes have cooled in the pan for five minutes, move them to a wire rack to finish cooling.

Spanish Doughnuts

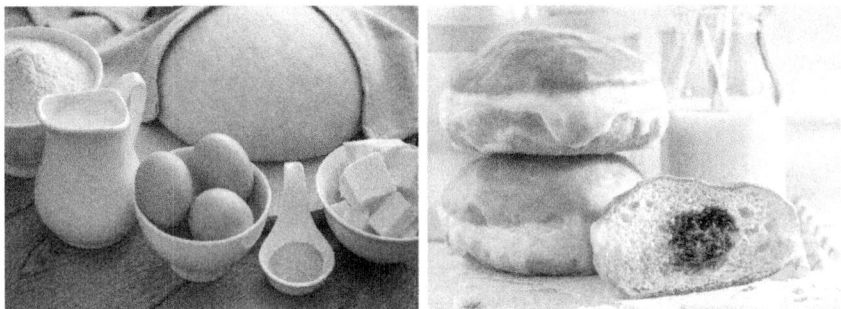

Ingredients:

- 2 cups all-purpose flour
- 2 teaspoons baking powder
- 1/2 teaspoon salt
- 1/4 cup sugar
- 2 tablespoons unsalted butter, melted
- 2 eggs
- 1/2 cup milk
- Oil for frying
- Sugar for coating

Instructions:

1. Combine the flour, sugar, baking powder, and salt in a bowl.
2. Whisk the eggs, milk, and melted butter in a separate basin.

3. Stir the dry ingredients into the wet mixture gradually until a dough forms.
4. Place the dough on a floured surface and give it a quick knead until it's smooth.
5. Use a glass or a doughnut cutter to cut the dough into circles after rolling it out to a thickness of 1/2 inch.
6. Preheat the oil in a big skillet or deep fryer to 180°C (350°F).
7. Fry the doughnuts in batches for two to three minutes on each side or until golden brown.
8. While still warm, drain on paper towels and roll in sugar.
9. Present the heated doughnuts.

Spanish Cheesecake

Ingredients:

- 250g cream cheese, softened
- 1/2 cup sugar
- 2 eggs
- 1 teaspoon vanilla extract
- Zest of 1 lemon
- 1/4 cup sour cream
- Graham cracker crust (store-bought or homemade)

Instructions:

1. Set the oven temperature to 160°C (325°F).
2. Beat the cream cheese and sugar together in a bowl until creamy.
3. One egg at a time, adding and beating thoroughly after each addition.
4. Add the sour cream, lemon zest, and vanilla essence and stir until thoroughly blended.

5. Fill the prepared graham cracker crust with the ingredients.
6. Bake for 40 to 45 minutes, or until the centre still has some give and the borders are set.
7. After turning off the oven, leave the door ajar for an hour to allow the cheesecake to cool within.
8. Before serving, let the cheesecake cool in the fridge for at least four hours or overnight.

Fig Bread

Ingredients:

- 2 cups dried figs, chopped
- 1/2 cup water
- 1/4 cup honey
- 1/4 cup orange juice
- 2 cups all-purpose flour
- 1 teaspoon baking powder
- 1/2 teaspoon baking soda
- 1/4 teaspoon salt
- 1/2 cup unsalted butter, softened
- 1/2 cup brown sugar
- 2 eggs
- 1 teaspoon vanilla extract
- 1/2 cup chopped nuts (optional)

Instructions:

1. Set the oven temperature to 180°C or 350°F. Oil and dust a loaf pan.
2. Put the chopped figs, water, honey, and orange juice in a saucepan. After ten minutes of simmering over low heat, could you turn off the heat and allow it to cool?

3. Combine the flour, baking soda, baking powder, and salt in a basin.
4. Cream the butter and brown sugar in a separate bowl until the mixture is light and fluffy.
5. Stir in the vanilla essence after beating in each egg one at a time.
6. Mix until just incorporated, and gradually add the dry ingredients to the wet components.
7. If using, fold in the chopped nuts and the fig combination.
8. Transfer the mixture to the loaf pan that has been ready and level the top.
9. Bake for fifty to sixty minutes or until a toothpick inserted in the middle comes out clean.
10. After the bread has cooled in the pan for ten minutes, move it to a wire rack to finish cooling.

Chocolate Palmiers

Ingredients:

- 1 sheet puff pastry, thawed
- 1/2 cup chocolate chips
- 1 egg, beaten (for egg wash)
- Sugar for sprinkling

Instructions:

1. Set the oven temperature to 200°C or 400°F. Use parchment paper to line a baking sheet.
2. Using a surface dusted with flour, roll out the puff pastry sheet to create a rectangle.
3. Evenly distribute the chocolate pieces throughout the pastry.

4. Tightly roll the pastry toward the centre, starting at one long edge. To ensure that both rolls meet in the centre, repeat with the other long edge.
5. Cut the rolled pastry into slices that are 1/2 inch thick.
6. Lay the slices, cut side down, on the baking sheet that has been prepared.
7. Dust the palmiers' tops with sugar after brushing them with beaten eggs.
8. Bake for 15 to 20 minutes or until crisp and golden brown.
9. Let cool for a few minutes on the baking sheet, then move to a wire rack to finish cooling.

Spanish Flan

Ingredients:

- 1 cup sugar
- 4 eggs
- 2 cups whole milk
- 1 teaspoon vanilla extract

Instructions:

1. Set oven temperature to 175°C/350°F.
2. Melt sugar in a small saucepan over medium heat, stirring regularly, until golden brown. Spoon caramelized sugar into individual ramekins or a flan mould, tilting to coat the bottom equally.
3. Beat eggs in a mixing basin with milk and vanilla essence. Blend until thoroughly blended.
4. Transfer the egg mixture into ramekins or a mould coated in caramel.
5. To create a water bath, place the mould or ramekins in a baking dish filled with hot water.

6. Bake the flan for 45 to 50 minutes, or until it sets, in the preheated oven.
7. Take it out of the oven and let it cool. Allow to cool for a minimum of two hours prior to serving.
8. To serve, flip the mould or ramekins onto a serving plate by running a knife around their edges.

Wine Cookies

Ingredients:

- 2 cups all-purpose flour
- 1/2 cup sugar
- 1/2 cup white wine
- Zest of 1 lemon
- 1/2 cup olive oil
- 1 teaspoon baking powder
- Pinch of salt
- Powdered sugar for dusting

Instructions:

1. Preheat oven to 350°F (175°C) and line a baking sheet with parchment paper.
2. In a mixing bowl, combine flour, sugar, lemon zest, baking powder, and salt.
3. Gradually add white wine and olive oil to the dry ingredients, mixing until a dough forms.
4. Roll the dough into small balls and then shape them into rings.
5. Place the rings onto the prepared baking sheet and bake for about 15-20 minutes or until they are lightly golden.
6. Remove from the oven and let them cool slightly.
7. Dust the cookies with powdered sugar before serving.

Sweet Spiral Pastries

Ingredients:

- 4 cups all-purpose flour
- 1/2 cup sugar
- 1/2 cup warm milk
- 1/2 cup melted butter
- 2 eggs
- 1 tablespoon active dry yeast
- Zest of 1 lemon
- Pinch of salt
- Powdered sugar for dusting

Instructions:

1. In a small basin, dissolve the yeast in the warm milk and leave it for about five minutes or until frothy.
2. Combine flour, sugar, lemon zest, and salt in a sizable mixing bowl.
3. Create a well in the middle of the dry ingredients and pour in the eggs, melted butter, and yeast mixture.
4. Mix until dough forms, then knead until smooth and elastic, for about 10 minutes on a floured surface.
5. After the dough has doubled in size, please place it in an oiled bowl, cover it with a fresh kitchen towel, and let it rise in a warm location for one to two hours.
6. Break the dough into little pieces by punching it down.
7. Create a thin rectangle out of each part, then roll it into a spiral.
8. Transfer the spirals to a parchment-lined baking sheet, cover with a kitchen towel, and leave to rise for another thirty to forty-five minutes.
9. Set oven temperature to 175°C/350°F.

10. Bake the ensaimadas until they are golden brown, 15 to 20 minutes.
11. Take them out of the oven and give them a little time to cool down before sprinkling with powdered sugar.

Spanish Shortbread Cookies

Ingredients:

- 2 cups all-purpose flour
- 1 cup powdered sugar
- 1 cup unsalted butter, softened
- 1/2 cup ground almonds
- 1 teaspoon vanilla extract
- Pinch of salt

Instructions:

1. Preheat the oven to 350°F (175°C), and place parchment paper on a baking pan.
2. Combine powdered sugar and softened butter in a mixing bowl and beat until smooth.
3. Until a dough forms, gradually add the flour, ground almonds, vanilla essence, and salt to the butter mixture and stir.
4. Form the dough into little balls and arrange them on the ready baking sheet.
5. Use the palm of your hand to flatten each ball softly.
6. Bake until the sides are just beginning to turn brown, 12 to 15 minutes.
7. Take the cookies out of the oven and allow them to cool for a few minutes on the baking sheet before moving them to a wire rack to finish cooling.

Fried Milk Dessert

Ingredients:

- 4 cups whole milk
- 1 cup sugar
- 1/2 cup cornstarch
- Zest of 1 lemon
- Cinnamon sticks
- 2 eggs, beaten
- Bread crumbs
- Olive oil for frying
- Powdered sugar for dusting

Instructions:

1. Place the milk, sugar, lemon zest, and cinnamon sticks in a saucepan and cook over medium heat until the mixture begins to simmer. Remove the pan from the heat and let it cool a little.
2. To make a slurry, combine cornstarch and a small amount of water in a bowl.
3. Stir the cornstarch slurry into the heated milk mixture gradually until it thickens.
4. Transfer the mixture to a square baking dish after removing the cinnamon sticks. Using a spatula, level the top and refrigerate for several hours or overnight to let it cool completely.
5. After the milk mixture has hardened, cut it into rectangles or squares.
6. Coat each piece in bread crumbs after dipping it into beaten eggs.
7. In a frying pan, heat the olive oil over medium heat.

8. Fry the coated milk pieces until both sides are golden brown.
9. Take out the oil and place it on paper towels to drain.
10. Sprinkle with powdered sugar prior to serving hot.

Anise and Brandy Pastries

Ingredients:

- 2 cups all-purpose flour
- 1/2 cup sugar
- 1/2 cup olive oil
- 1/2 cup brandy
- 1/4 cup anise seeds
- Zest of 1 orange
- Pinch of salt
- Powdered sugar for dusting

Instructions:

1. Combine flour, sugar, orange zest, anise seeds, and salt in a mixing bowl.
2. Mix the dry ingredients with the brandy and olive oil gradually until a dough forms.
3. Using a surface dusted with flour, roll out the dough and cut it into tiny rectangles.
4. Cut a tiny hole in the middle of each rectangle, then thread one end through to tie a knot.
5. In a frying pan, heat the olive oil over medium heat.
6. Fry the pastries in batches until both sides are golden brown.
7. Take out the oil and place it on paper towels to drain.
8. Before serving, dust with powdered sugar.

Sweet Bread with Candied Fruits

Ingredients:

- 4 cups all-purpose flour
- 1/2 cup sugar
- 1/2 cup olive oil
- 1/2 cup warm water
- 1/4 cup orange juice
- 1/4 cup diced candied fruits (such as orange, lemon, or cherries)
- Zest of 1 lemon
- 1 packet of active dry yeast
- Pinch of salt
- Powdered sugar for dusting

Instructions:

1. Dissolve the yeast in warm water in a small basin and leave it for about five minutes or until frothy.
2. Combine flour, sugar, lemon zest, and salt in a mixing basin.
3. Create a well in the middle of the dry ingredients and pour in the orange juice, olive oil, and yeast mixture.
4. Mix until dough forms, then knead until smooth and elastic, for about 10 minutes on a floured surface.
5. After the dough has doubled in size, please place it in an oiled bowl, cover it with a fresh kitchen towel, and let it rise in a warm location for one to two hours.
6. Break the dough into smaller pieces by punching it down.
7. Using parchment paper, line a baking sheet, then roll out each portion into a flat oval form.
8. Spread the dough with diced candied fruits.
9. Set oven temperature to 190°C/375°F.

10. Bake the sweetbreads until they are golden brown, about 20 to 25 minutes.
11. Take them out of the oven and let them cool slightly before sprinkling them with powdered sugar.

CHAPTER - 3
MORNING TREATS AND PASTRIES

Churro French Toast Sticks

Ingredients:

- Bread slices
- Eggs
- Milk
- Sugar
- Cinnamon
- Vegetable oil

Instructions:

1. Slice bread into sticks.
2. Combine the eggs, milk, sugar, and cinnamon in a bowl.
3. Submerge bread sticks in the beaten egg.
4. Fry till golden brown in vegetable oil.
5. Top with maple syrup or chocolate sauce.

Spanish Omelette Muffins

Ingredients:

- Eggs
- Potatoes
- Onion
- Olive oil
- Salt

Instructions:

1. Peel and cut the onion and potatoes.
2. In olive oil, fry potatoes and onion till golden.
3. In a bowl, beat the eggs and add salt.
4. Mix the eggs with the cooked potatoes and onion.
5. Fill muffin pans with mixture.
6. Bake for a predetermined time.

Almond Cake

Ingredients:

- Almond flour
- Sugar
- Eggs
- Lemon zest
- Cinnamon
- Butter

Instructions:

1. Combine almond flour, sugar, eggs, cinnamon, and lemon zest.
2. Transfer to an oiled cake tin.
3. Bake until browned and golden.

4. Before serving, dust with powdered sugar.

Spanish Breakfast Bread Pudding

Ingredients:

- Bread slices
- Milk
- Eggs
- Sugar
- Vanilla extract
- Cinnamon
- Raisins (optional)

Instructions:

1. Preheat oven to 350°F (175°C).
2. Tear bread slices into pieces and place in a greased baking dish.
3. In a bowl, whisk together milk, eggs, sugar, vanilla extract, and cinnamon.
4. Pour the mixture over the bread, ensuring it's evenly soaked.
5. Sprinkle raisins over the top if desired.
6. Bake for about 30-35 minutes or until set and golden brown.

Sweet Bread

Ingredients for the Dough:

- All-purpose flour
- Sugar
- Active dry yeast
- Milk

- Butter
- Eggs
- Vanilla extract
- Salt

Ingredients for the Topping:

- All-purpose flour
- Sugar
- Butter
- Vanilla extract
- Food coloring (optional)

Instructions:

1. To make a dough, combine flour, sugar, yeast, eggs, melted butter, warm milk, vanilla essence, and salt in a bowl.
2. Allow the dough to rise until it doubles in size after kneading it until it is smooth and elastic.
3. Shape the dough into spheres and arrange them onto a baking tray.
4. To make the topping, sift together flour, sugar, butter, and vanilla essence. Add food colouring for added colour.
5. After rolling out the topping, cover the dough balls.
6. Score the topping with a knife to create artistic lines.
7. After letting the conchas rise for an additional 30 minutes, bake them for 20 to 25 minutes, or until golden brown, at 350°F (175°C).

Spanish Almond Croissants

Ingredients:

- Croissant dough (store-bought or homemade)
- Almond paste or marzipan
- Sliced almonds
- Powdered sugar (optional)

Instructions:

1. Roll out croissant dough into triangles.
2. Place a small amount of almond paste or marzipan on each triangle and roll up.
3. Brush with egg wash and sprinkle sliced almonds on top.
4. Bake according to the croissant dough instructions.
5. Dust with powdered sugar before serving if desired.

Cream-filled Empanadas

Ingredients for the Dough:

- All-purpose flour
- Butter
- Salt
- Cold water

Ingredients for the Filling:

- Pastry cream (store-bought or homemade)
- Powdered sugar for dusting (optional)

Instructions:

1. Crumble together flour, butter, and salt in a bowl.

2. Add chilly water little by little until the dough comes together.
3. Cut the dough into rounds after rolling it out.
4. In the centre of each circle, place a tablespoon of pastry cream.
5. Using a fork, crimp the edges of the half-moon-shaped dough after folding it over.
6. Transfer to a baking sheet and bake for 20 to 25 minutes, or until golden brown, at 375°F (190°C).
7. If preferred, sprinkle with powdered sugar prior to serving.

Chocolatey Churro Croissants

Ingredients:

- Croissant dough (store-bought or homemade)
- Chocolate hazelnut spread
- Cinnamon sugar

Instructions:

1. Form triangles out of croissant dough.
2. Cover each triangle with a chocolate hazelnut spread.
3. Form the triangles into croissant shapes by rolling them up.
4. Bake as directed by the croissant dough recipe.
5. While still warm, sprinkle with cinnamon sugar.

Olive Oil Biscuits

Ingredients:

- All-purpose flour
- Olive oil
- Sugar
- Anise seeds
- White wine
- Lemon zest
- Salt

Instructions:

1. Mix flour, olive oil, sugar, anise seeds, white wine, lemon zest, and salt to form a dough.
2. Roll out the dough thinly and cut into rounds or shapes.
3. Place on a baking sheet and bake at 350°F (175°C) for 12-15 minutes or until lightly golden.
4. Serve as a sweet snack or breakfast treat.

Spanish Orange Blossom Muffins

Ingredients:

- All-purpose flour
- Sugar
- Baking powder
- Salt
- Milk
- Vegetable oil
- Orange blossom water
- Eggs
- Orange zest

Instructions:

1. Warm up the oven to 375°F (190°C) and coat muffin tins with oil.
2. Combine flour, sugar, baking powder, and salt in a sizable bowl.
3. Combine milk, vegetable oil, orange blossom water, eggs, and orange zest in a separate bowl.
4. Just mix the dry and wet components.
5. Fill muffin cups to the brim with batter, and bake for 18 to 20 minutes, or until a toothpick inserted in the middle comes out clean.
6. Let cool completely before serving.

Anise Donuts

Ingredients:

- All-purpose flour
- Sugar
- Baking powder
- Salt
- Anise seeds
- Milk
- Eggs
- Butter
- Vegetable oil (for frying)
- Powdered sugar (for dusting)

Instructions:

1. Put the flour, sugar, baking powder, salt, and anise seeds in a bowl.
2. Whisk the milk, eggs, and melted butter in another basin.

3. Mix the dry ingredients thoroughly after progressively adding the wet ingredients.
4. Preheat 350°F (175°C) vegetable oil in a deep fryer or large pot.
5. Drop dough spoonfuls into the heated oil and cook for two to three minutes on each side or until golden brown.
6. Take out the oil and place it on paper towels to drain.
7. Before serving, dust with powdered sugar.

Spanish Pastry

Ingredients for the Dough:

- All-purpose flour
- Sugar
- Salt
- Active dry yeast
- Warm water
- Olive oil

Ingredients for the Topping:

- Tomatoes
- Olive oil
- Garlic
- Salt
- Fresh herbs (such as thyme or rosemary)

Instructions:

1. To make the dough, combine the flour, sugar, salt, yeast, warm water, and olive oil in a bowl.
2. Allow the dough to rise until it doubles in size after kneading it until it is smooth and elastic.
3. Set oven temperature to 200°C/400°F.

4. After rolling out the dough, transfer it to a baking sheet.
5. Cut tomatoes into thin slices and place them over the dough.
6. Add a drizzle of olive oil and season with salt, fresh herbs, and chopped garlic.
7. Bake for twenty to twenty-five minutes or until the crust is browned.
8. You can serve it warm or cold.

Spanish Lemon Polenta Cake

Ingredients:

- Butter
- Sugar
- Eggs
- Lemon zest
- Lemon juice
- Almond flour
- Polenta (cornmeal)
- Baking powder
- Salt

Instructions:

1. Preheat the oven to 350°F (175°C), and coat a cake pan with oil.
2. Beat sugar and butter together until frothy and light.
3. Add the lemon zest and juice after beating in the eggs one at a time.
4. Combine almond flour, polenta, baking powder, and salt in another basin.
5. Mix the dry ingredients thoroughly after progressively adding them to the wet components.

6. Transfer the mixture to the ready cake tin and level the top.
7. Bake the cake for thirty to thirty-five minutes or until a toothpick inserted in the centre comes out clean.
8. Let cool completely before serving.

Spanish Shortbread

Ingredients:

- All-purpose flour
- Powdered sugar
- Ground almonds
- Butter
- Lemon zest
- Cinnamon

Instructions:

1. Preheat the oven to 350°F (175°C), and place parchment paper on a baking pan.
2. Combine flour, cinnamon, ground almonds, powdered sugar, and lemon zest in a bowl.
3. Until the mixture resembles coarse crumbs, cut in butter.
4. Roll the dough into disks or form it into tiny balls.
5. Transfer to the baking sheet that has been prepared, and bake for 12 to 15 minutes or until lightly golden.
6. Let cool completely before serving.

Crema Catalana Cinnamon Rolls

Ingredients for the Dough:

- All-purpose flour
- Sugar
- Active dry yeast
- Milk
- Butter
- Eggs
- Salt

Ingredients for the Filling:

- Brown sugar
- Cinnamon
- Butter

Ingredients for the Glaze:

- Powdered sugar
- Milk
- Vanilla extract

Instructions:

1. To make the dough, combine the flour, sugar, yeast, warm milk, melted butter, eggs, and salt in a basin.
2. Allow the dough to rise until it doubles in size after kneading it until it is smooth and elastic.
3. Create a rectangle shape out of the dough.
4. Cover the dough with melted butter and then top with cinnamon and brown sugar.
5. Tightly roll the dough and cut it into slices.

6. After placing the slices on a baking tray that has been oiled, give them 30 minutes to rise.
7. Bake for 20 to 25 minutes, or until golden brown, at 375°F (190°C).
8. To prepare the glaze, combine the powdered sugar, milk, and vanilla essence in a small basin.
9. Before serving, drizzle the glaze over the cinnamon rolls.

CHAPTER - 4
CLASSIC SPANISH BREAD RECIPES

Pan de Higo (Fig Bread)

Ingredients:

- 300g dried figs
- 100g almonds
- 50g walnuts
- 50g hazelnuts
- 50g pistachios
- 50g pine nuts
- 1 teaspoon ground cinnamon
- 1/2 teaspoon ground cloves
- 1/4 teaspoon ground nutmeg
- 1/4 teaspoon ground black pepper
- 1 tablespoon honey
- Zest of 1 orange
- Zest of 1 lemon

Instructions:

1. Finely chop the pine nuts, pistachios, almonds, walnuts, and hazelnuts.
2. Place the chopped nuts and figs in a big basin and toss to blend with the honey, orange and lemon zest, cloves, nutmeg, ground cinnamon, and black pepper.
3. Firmly press the mixture into a parchment paper-lined loaf pan.
4. Place plastic wrap over the pan and place it in the refrigerator to firm it up for at least two hours.
5. After the fig bread hardens, take it out of the loaf pan and cut it into thin pieces to serve.

Spanish Olive Oil Bread

Ingredients:

- 500g bread flour
- 10g salt
- 10g sugar
- 25g fresh yeast
- 250ml warm water
- 100ml Spanish extra virgin olive oil

Instructions:

1. Place the sugar, salt, and bread flour in a sizable mixing basin.
2. Add the fresh yeast and olive oil to the flour mixture after dissolving it in the warm water.
3. Mix until a dough forms, then knead the dough for about ten minutes, or until it is smooth and elastic, on a surface dusted with flour.

4. After the dough has doubled in size, please place it in a greased bowl, cover it with a fresh kitchen towel, and let it rise in a warm location for about an hour.
5. Turn the oven on to 200°C, or 400°F.
6. Form the risen dough into a loaf or rolls by pressing it down.
7. Place the formed dough on a parchment-lined baking sheet and let it rise for an additional thirty minutes.
8. Bake for 25 to 30 minutes, or until golden brown, in a preheated oven.
9. Before serving, let the bread cool somewhat.

Catalan Flatbread

Ingredients:

- 500g bread flour
- 10g salt
- 10g sugar
- 25g fresh yeast
- 250ml warm water
- 50ml Spanish extra virgin olive oil
- Toppings of choice (e.g., tomatoes, onions, peppers, olives)

Instructions:

1. To make the dough, proceed as directed for Pan de Aceite.
2. Set oven temperature to 220°C (425°F).
3. Using a baking sheet covered with parchment paper, divide the dough into smaller sections and form them into flat rounds.
4. Apply your preferred toppings to the tops of the dough rounds after brushing them with olive oil.

5. Bake for 15 to 20 minutes, or until crispy and golden brown, in a preheated oven.
6. Offer hot or room temperature.

Spanish Glass Bread

Ingredients:

- 500g bread flour
- 10g salt
- 10g sugar
- 25g fresh yeast
- 250ml warm water
- 50ml Spanish extra virgin olive oil

Instructions:

1. Place the sugar, salt, and bread flour in a sizable mixing basin.
2. Add the fresh yeast and olive oil to the flour mixture after dissolving it in the warm water.
3. Mix until a dough forms, then knead the dough for about ten minutes, or until it is smooth and elastic, on a surface dusted with flour.
4. After the dough has doubled in size, please place it in a greased bowl, cover it with a fresh kitchen towel, and let it rise in a warm location for about an hour.
5. Set a baking stone or inverted baking sheet inside the oven to preheat as you preheat the oven to 220°C (425°F).
6. Divide the risen dough into two halves by punching it down.
7. On a surface dusted with flour, roll out each slice of dough into a thin rectangle.

8. Gently place the dough that has been rolled out onto parchment paper.
9. Place the parchment paper containing the dough onto the baking sheet or stone that has been warmed in the oven.
10. Bake for ten to fifteen minutes or until the bread is crispy and golden brown.
11. Take it out of the oven and give it a little time to cool before serving.

Three Kings Cake

Ingredients:

- 500g bread flour
- 100g sugar
- 10g salt
- 25g fresh yeast
- 100ml warm milk
- 100g unsalted butter, softened
- Zest of 1 orange
- Zest of 1 lemon
- 3 large eggs
- 1 tablespoon orange blossom water
- Candied fruits for decoration
- Sugar crystals or pearl sugar for decoration

Instructions:

1. Place the bread flour, sugar, and salt in a large mixing bowl.
2. Add the fresh yeast to the flour mixture after dissolving it in the heated milk.
3. Fill the bowl with the eggs, orange blossom water, softened butter, and lemon and orange zest.

4. Mix until a dough forms, then knead the dough for about ten minutes, or until it is smooth and elastic, on a surface dusted with flour.
5. After the dough has doubled in size, please place it in an oiled bowl, cover it with a fresh kitchen towel, and let it rise in a warm location for one to two hours.
6. Form the risen dough into a ring by pressing it down.
7. Set the dough ring on a parchment paper-lined baking sheet.
8. Use sugar crystals or pearl sugar and candied fruits to decorate the dough's top.
9. Let the dough rest for a further thirty to forty-five minutes, loosely covered with plastic wrap.
10. Turn the oven on to 180°C or 350°F.
11. In a preheated oven, bake the Roscon de Reyes for 25 to 30 minutes or until they are cooked through and golden brown.
12. Before serving, let the cake cool slightly.

Cadiz Bread

Ingredients:

- 500g all-purpose flour
- 10g salt
- 10g sugar
- 25g fresh yeast
- 250ml warm water
- 50ml Spanish extra virgin olive oil
- 100g chopped chorizo
- 100g chopped serrano ham
- 100g grated Manchego cheese

Instructions:

1. Place the sugar, salt, and all-purpose flour in a sizable mixing basin.
2. Add the fresh yeast and olive oil to the flour mixture after dissolving it in the warm water.
3. Mix until a dough forms, then knead the dough for about ten minutes, or until it is smooth and elastic, on a surface dusted with flour.
4. After the dough has doubled in size, please place it in a greased bowl, cover it with a fresh kitchen towel, and let it rise in a warm location for about an hour.
5. Turn the oven on to 200°C, or 400°F.
6. Divide the risen dough into two halves by punching it down.
7. Create a rectangle out of each piece of dough.
8. Top each dough rectangle with half of the grated Manchego cheese, chopped chorizo, and serrano ham.
9. Beginning with the long side, tightly roll up each dough rectangle.
10. After the dough has risen for 30 minutes, transfer it to a baking sheet covered with parchment paper.
11. Bake for 25 to 30 minutes, or until cooked through and golden brown, in a preheated oven.
12. Let the bread cool down a little before cutting it into slices and serving.

Mallorcan Pastry

Ingredients:

- 500g bread flour
- 10g salt
- 10g sugar

- 25g fresh yeast
- 250ml warm milk
- 100g unsalted butter, melted
- 100g sugar
- Powdered sugar for dusting

Instructions:

1. Place the sugar, salt, and bread flour in a sizable mixing basin.
2. Mix the melted butter and fresh yeast into the flour mixture after dissolving it in the heated milk.
3. Mix until a dough forms, then knead the dough for about ten minutes, or until it is smooth and elastic, on a surface dusted with flour.
4. After the dough has doubled in size, please place it in an oiled bowl, cover it with a fresh kitchen towel, and let it rise in a warm location for one to two hours.
5. Divide the risen dough into smaller pieces by punching it down.
6. Create a thin rectangle shape out of each slice of dough.
7. Create a tight spiral out of each dough rectangle.
8. Shape each dough spiral into a circle and arrange on a baking pan covered with parchment paper.
9. Give the dough rounds 30 to 45 more minutes to rise.
10. Turn the oven on to 180°C or 350°F.
11. Bake the Ensaimadas for 15 to 20 minutes, or until they are golden brown, in a preheated oven.
12. Allow the pastries to cool slightly before serving and sprinkling with powdered sugar.

Coca de San Juan (St. John's Cake)

Ingredients:

- 500g bread flour
- 15g fresh yeast
- 50ml olive oil
- 250ml warm water
- 10g salt
- 50g sugar
- Zest of 1 lemon
- 1 egg yolk
- Assorted fruits for topping (like cherries, figs, or apricots)
- Sugar for sprinkling

Instructions:

1. Dissolve the yeast in warm water and let it sit until foamy, for about 5 minutes.
2. Combine the flour, yeast mixture, lemon zest, sugar, salt, and olive oil in a sizable basin.
3. Work the dough into an elastic and smooth texture. In a warm environment, allow it to double in size for about an hour.
4. Turn the oven on to 200°C, or 400°F.
5. Form the dough into two equal sections by dividing it in half. Transfer them to a parchment paper-lined baking sheet.
6. Using your hands, slightly flatten each ball before adding the other fruits on top.
7. Dust the dough's edges with egg yolk and dust the fruits with sugar.
8. Bake for 20 to 25 minutes, or until golden brown, in a preheated oven.

9. Allow cakes to cool completely before slicing and serving.

Tomato Bread

Ingredients:

- 1 baguette or rustic bread loaf
- 2 ripe tomatoes
- 2 cloves garlic, peeled
- Extra virgin olive oil
- Salt

Instructions:

1. Thinly slice the bread and lightly toast it.
2. After cutting the tomatoes in half, grind them with a box grater on the coarse side, throwing away the skins.
3. Give the toast slices a gentle rub with the garlic cloves.
4. Top the bread pieces with the grated tomato and garlic rubbing.
5. Add a drizzle of olive oil and season with salt.
6. Present right away.

Tarta de Santiago (St. James' Cake)

Ingredients:

- 250g ground almonds
- 250g sugar
- 4 eggs
- Zest of 1 lemon
- Zest of 1 orange
- 1 tsp cinnamon
- Powdered sugar for dusting

Instructions:

1. Set the oven's temperature to 180°C (350°F). Line and grease a circular cake tin.
2. Beat the eggs and sugar in a bowl until the mixture is light and fluffy.
3. Until wholly blended, stir in the ground almonds, orange and lemon zests, and cinnamon.
4. Fill the cake tin with the mixture.
5. Bake for 30 to 40 minutes, or until firm and golden brown, in a preheated oven.
6. After the cake has cooled in the pan for ten minutes, move it to a wire rack to finish cooling.
7. Before serving, dust with powdered sugar.

Almond Bread

Ingredients:

- 500g bread flour
- 15g fresh yeast
- 250ml warm water
- 50g sugar
- 10g salt
- 100g ground almonds
- 50ml olive oil
- Sliced almonds for topping

Instructions:

1. Dissolve the yeast in warm water and let it sit until it is frothy, for about 5 minutes.
2. Combine the flour, sugar, salt, and ground almonds in a big bowl.

3. Combine the dry ingredients with the yeast mixture and olive oil. Stir to form a dough.
4. Work the dough until it is elastic and smooth, about ten minutes.
5. After the dough has doubled in size, please place it in a greased bowl, cover it with a fresh kitchen towel, and let it rise in a warm location for about an hour.
6. Turn the oven on to 200°C, or 400°F.
7. Form the risen dough into a loaf by pressing it down.
8. Transfer the loaf to a parchment paper-lined baking sheet.
9. Use water to lightly brush the top of the loaf and then top it with sliced almonds.
10. Bake for 25 to 30 minutes in a preheated oven or until the loaf is golden brown and hollow to the touch.
11. Before slicing and serving, allow the bread to cool on a wire rack.

Spanish Olive Oil Cake

Ingredients:

- 250g all-purpose flour
- 150ml extra virgin olive oil
- 150g sugar
- Zest of 1 lemon
- Zest of 1 orange
- 1 tsp anise seeds
- 1/2 tsp ground cinnamon
- 1/2 tsp ground cloves
- 1/2 tsp baking powder
- Pinch of salt

Instructions:

1. Set the oven's temperature to 180°C (350°F). Grease and dust a circular cake pan.
2. Combine the olive oil, sugar, orange and lemon zests, anise seeds, cinnamon, and cloves in a bowl.
3. Combine the flour, baking powder, and salt in another basin.
4. Add the dry ingredients to the wet components gradually and stir until thoroughly mixed.
5. Fill the cake tin with the batter.
6. In a preheated oven, bake for 30 to 35 minutes or until a toothpick inserted in the centre comes out clean.
7. After the cake has cooled in the pan for ten minutes, move it to a wire rack to finish cooling.
8. Present sliced and savoured!

Spanish Milk Bread

Ingredients:

- 500g bread flour
- 15g fresh yeast
- 250ml warm milk
- 50g sugar
- 50g unsalted butter, melted
- 1 egg
- 10g salt

Instructions:

1. Dissolve the yeast in the warm milk and let it sit until frothy, about 5 minutes.
2. Combine the flour, sugar, and salt in a sizable bowl.

3. Combine the dry ingredients with the melted butter, yeast mixture, and beaten egg. Stir to form a dough.
4. Work the dough until it is elastic and smooth, about ten minutes.
5. After the dough has doubled in size, please place it in a greased bowl, cover it with a fresh kitchen towel, and let it rise in a warm location for about an hour.
6. Turn the oven on to 180°C or 350°F.
7. Shape the risen dough into a loaf or rolls by pressing it down.
8. Transfer the dough to a parchment paper-lined baking sheet.
9. Give the dough another half an hour to rise.
10. Bake for 25 to 30 minutes (less if you're making rolls) in a preheated oven or until the loaf is golden brown and hollow to the touch.
11. Before slicing and serving, allow the bread to cool on a wire rack.

Spanish Easter Bread

Ingredients:

- 500g bread flour
- 15g fresh yeast
- 250ml warm water
- 100g chorizo, diced
- 100g bacon, diced
- 100g serrano ham, diced
- 1 onion, finely chopped
- 2 eggs
- Salt and pepper to taste
- Hard-boiled eggs for decoration (optional)

Instructions:

1. Dissolve the yeast in warm water and let it sit until it is frothy, for about 5 minutes.
2. Combine the flour and the salt in a large bowl.
3. Combine the flour and yeast mixture, kneading until a dough forms.
4. After the dough has doubled in size, cover it and let it rest in a warm location for about an hour.
5. In the interim, sauté an onion in a skillet with a bit of olive oil until it becomes transparent. Add the bacon, serrano ham, and sliced chorizo. Cook the meats until they take on colour. To taste, add salt and pepper for seasoning. Allow the blend to cool.
6. Turn the oven on to 180°C or 350°F.
7. Gently press the risen dough down and split it into two equal pieces.
8. Roll out every piece to form a rectangle.
9. Evenly cover one of the rectangles with the cooled beef mixture, leaving a border all the way around.
10. Cover with the remaining dough rectangle and press the sides together.
11. Transfer the dough to a parchment paper-lined baking sheet.
12. If preferred, garnish the top with hard-boiled eggs.
13. Bake for 30 to 35 minutes, or until golden brown, in an oven that has been warmed.
14. Before slicing and serving, allow the bread to cool on a wire rack.

Catalan Vegetable Pastry

Ingredients:

- 500g bread flour
- 15g fresh yeast
- 250ml warm water
- 50ml olive oil
- 10g salt
- Assorted vegetables (bell peppers, onions, tomatoes, eggplant, etc.)
- Salt and pepper to taste
- Optional: anchovies, olives

Instructions:

1. Dissolve the yeast in warm water and let it sit until it is frothy, for about 5 minutes.
2. Combine the flour, olive oil, and salt in a sizable bowl.
3. Combine the dry ingredients with the yeast mixture and knead until a dough forms.
4. After the dough has doubled in size, cover it and let it rest in a warm location for about an hour.
5. Meanwhile, thinly slice the vegetables.
6. Turn the oven on to 200°C, or 400°F.
7. Divide the risen dough into parts by punching it down.
8. Roll out each piece to form a slender circle or rectangle.
9. Transfer the dough to a parchment paper-lined baking sheet.
10. Place the cut veggies on top of the dough, encircling the edges with a border.
11. Season with pepper and salt, and feel free to add extras like olives or anchovies.

12. In a preheated oven, bake for 20 to 25 minutes or until the crust is crispy and golden brown.
13. Before cutting and serving, allow the pastry to cool somewhat.

CHAPTER - 5
SWEET DELIGHTS: CAKES AND TARTS

Basque Cake

Ingredients:

- 250g unsalted butter, softened
- 250g granulated sugar
- 4 eggs
- 250g all-purpose flour
- 1 tsp baking powder
- Zest of 1 lemon
- Zest of 1 orange
- 1 tsp vanilla extract
- 100g ground almonds
- 100g pastry cream

Instructions:

1. Set the oven's temperature to 180°C (350°F). Coat a 9-inch cake pan with flour and butter.
2. Cream the butter and sugar in a mixing bowl until the mixture is light and fluffy.
3. Add the eggs one at a time, thoroughly combining each time.

4. Add the vanilla extract and orange and lemon zests, and stir.
5. Fold the flour and baking powder into the mixture until just incorporated after sifting them together.
6. Stir in the almond meal.
7. Fill the cake pan with half of the batter.
8. Evenly distribute the pastry cream throughout the batter.
9. Apply the remaining batter on top.
10. Cook for forty to forty-five minutes or until a toothpick inserted in the centre comes out clean.
11. Let cool completely before serving.

Roscon de Reyes (King's Cake)

Ingredients:

- 500g all-purpose flour
- 100g granulated sugar
- 100g unsalted butter, softened
- 3 eggs
- 1/2 cup warm milk
- 25g fresh yeast
- Zest of 1 lemon
- Zest of 1 orange
- 1 tsp orange blossom water
- 1 tsp rum (optional)
- Candied fruits (for decoration)
- Slivered almonds (for decoration)
- Powdered sugar (for dusting)

Instructions:

1. Dissolve the yeast in the warm milk in a small basin.
2. Place the flour and sugar in a sizable mixing bowl.

3. Stir in the eggs, butter, yeast mixture, orange and lemon zests, orange blossom water, and rum, if using.
4. Mix to make a dough, then knead until smooth and elastic on a surface dusted with flour.
5. Transfer the dough to a greased basin, cover it with a fresh kitchen towel, and let it rest for one to two hours in a warm location until it has doubled in size.
6. Press the dough into a ring shape and transfer it to a parchment paper-lined baking sheet.
7. Add slivered almonds and candied fruits on the top.
8. Place a fresh kitchen towel over it and wait 30 to 45 minutes for it to rise once more.
9. Turn the oven on to 180°C or 350°F.
10. Bake for 25 to 30 minutes or until the cake is golden brown.
11. Let it cool before dusting it with powdered sugar.

Spanish Apple Cake

Ingredients:

- 3-4 large apples, peeled, cored, and sliced
- 200g all-purpose flour
- 150g granulated sugar
- 100g unsalted butter, melted
- 2 eggs
- 1 tsp baking powder
- 1 tsp vanilla extract
- Pinch of salt
- Powdered sugar (for dusting)

Instructions:

1. Set the oven's temperature to 180°C (350°F). Coat a 9-inch cake pan with flour and butter.
2. Gently whisk the eggs, sugar, vanilla extract, melted butter, and salt in a mixing bowl until thoroughly blended.
3. Add the flour and baking powder gradually and stir until smooth.
4. Fill the cake pan with the batter.
5. Place the apple slices in a circle on top of the batter.
6. Bake for 35 to 40 minutes, or until the middle of the cake is clean when a toothpick is inserted and the cake is golden brown.
7. Let it cool before adding a powdered sugar coating.

Mallorcan Sweet Pastry

Ingredients:

- 500g bread flour
- 200ml warm milk
- 100g granulated sugar
- 2 eggs
- 100g unsalted butter, softened
- 10g active dry yeast
- Pinch of salt
- Powdered sugar (for dusting)

Instructions:

1. In a small bowl, dissolve the yeast and a teaspoon of sugar in the warm milk. Allow it to sit until foamy, about 5 minutes.

2. Combine the flour, salt, eggs, softened butter, and the remaining sugar in a sizable mixing basin.
3. Add the yeast mixture and knead the dough until it becomes smooth.
4. Place a fresh kitchen towel over the dough and let it rest in a warm location until it has doubled in size, around one to two hours.
5. Turn the oven on to 180°C or 350°F.
6. Break the dough into smaller pieces by punching it down.
7. Roll out each piece to form a slender rectangle.
8. For each rectangle into a coil by rolling it up into a tight spiral.
9. Arrange the coils, with space between them, on a baking sheet covered with parchment paper.
10. Give the coils another 30 to 45 minutes to rise.
11. Bake until golden brown, 15 to 20 minutes.
12. Let it cool before dusting it with powdered sugar.

Chocolate Orange Cake

Ingredients:

- 200g dark chocolate, chopped
- 150g unsalted butter
- 150g granulated sugar
- 4 eggs
- Zest of 1 orange
- 100g all-purpose flour
- 1 tsp baking powder
- Pinch of salt
- Powdered sugar (for dusting)

Instructions:

1. Set the oven's temperature to 180°C (350°F). Coat a 9-inch cake pan with flour and butter.
2. Melt the butter and chocolate in a heatproof bowl over a double boiler or in the microwave. Blend until a smooth consistency is achieved.
3. Beat the eggs, sugar, and orange zest in a mixing bowl until light and fluffy.
4. Add the melted chocolate mixture gradually while stirring to incorporate it.
5. Fold in the salt, baking powder, and flour slowly until just mixed. Sift in.
6. Fill the cake pan with the batter.
7. Bake for 25 to 30 minutes, or until a toothpick inserted into the centre comes out with moist crumbs.
8. Let it cool before sprinkling it with powdered sugar.

Spanish Swiss Roll

Ingredients:

- 4 eggs
- 100g granulated sugar
- 100g all-purpose flour
- 1 tsp vanilla extract
- 200g dulce de leche or jam of your choice
- Powdered sugar (for dusting)

Instructions:

1. Set the oven to 180°C (350°F). Grease and line a 9 x 13-inch baking tray with parchment paper.
2. Beat the eggs and granulated sugar in a sizable mixing bowl until light and frothy.

3. Include the vanilla essence and stir to incorporate.
4. Fold the flour mixture carefully until no lumps are left after sifting it into the egg mixture.
5. Transfer the batter to the baking tray that has been ready and level it out.
6. Bake for ten to twelve minutes or until the sponge is brown and pliable to the touch.
7. Gently place the heated sponge onto a fresh tea towel that has been sprinkled with powdered sugar.
8. Remove the parchment paper and, if needed, trim the sponge's edges.
9. Evenly distribute the jam or dulce de leche over the sponge.
10. Roll the sponge tightly from one short end to the other, using the tea towel for support.
11. Arrange the rolled sponge on a serving plate, seam side down.
12. Before serving, dust with powdered sugar.

Spanish Lemon Tart

Ingredients:

- 200g all-purpose flour
- 100g unsalted butter, cold and diced
- 50g granulated sugar
- 1 egg yolk
- Pinch of salt

For the lemon filling:

- 4 large eggs
- 150g granulated sugar
- Zest and juice of 3 lemons

- 150ml heavy cream

Instructions:

1. Set the oven's temperature to 180°C (350°F). Butter and dust a 9-inch pie tin.
2. Pulse the flour, chilled butter, sugar, egg yolk, and salt in a food processor until the mixture resembles fine breadcrumbs.
3. Evenly press the mixture into the tart pan, covering the edges and bottom.
4. After using a fork to pierce the base, refrigerate for half an hour.
5. Bake the tart shell for 15 minutes without a blind bake, then take off the weights and bake for a further 5 minutes or until brown.
6. Make the lemon filling while the tart shell bakes. In a bowl, beat the eggs, sugar, lemon zest juice, heavy cream, and lemon juice until creamy.
7. Fill the baked tart shell with the lemon filling.
8. Put the tart back in the oven and bake it for another twenty to twenty-five minutes or until the filling is set.
9. Let the tart cool thoroughly before cutting into slices and serving.

Spanish Sponge Cake Roll

Ingredients:

- 4 large eggs
- 1/2 cup granulated sugar
- 1/2 cup all-purpose flour
- 1 teaspoon vanilla extract
- Powdered sugar for dusting

- Jam or dulce de leche (optional for filling)

Instructions:

1. Set the oven's temperature to 175°C/350°F. Grease and line a jelly roll pan (10 x 15 inches) with parchment paper.
2. Beat the eggs and granulated sugar in a sizable mixing bowl for approximately five minutes or until the mixture is pale and thick.
3. Until just mixed, gently fold in the flour and vanilla extract.
4. Evenly distribute the batter in the pan that has been prepared.
5. Bake for ten to twelve minutes or until the cake bounces back when you touch it and is gently yellow.
6. Use a knife to gently release the cake's edges while it's still warm, then flip it over onto a fresh kitchen towel sprinkled with powdered sugar.
7. Remove the parchment paper and tightly roll the cake and cloth together.
8. Allow the rolled cake to cool fully.
9. Unroll the cake, spread dulce de leche or jam on it if you'd like, and then roll it back up without the towel.
10. Before serving, dust with powdered sugar. Cut and savour!

Almond Chocolate Tart

Ingredients:

- 1 9-inch pie crust, baked and cooled
- 1 cup almond meal
- 1/2 cup granulated sugar

- 1/4 cup unsweetened cocoa powder
- 2 large eggs
- 1/2 cup heavy cream
- 1 teaspoon almond extract
- 1/2 cup sliced almonds, toasted (for garnish)
- Powdered sugar (for dusting)

Instructions:

1. Set the oven's temperature to 175°C/350°F.
2. Put cocoa powder, granulated sugar, and almond meal in a sizable mixing basin.
3. Include almond extract, heavy cream, and eggs. Blend until thoroughly blended.
4. Evenly distribute the mixture throughout the prepared pie shell.
5. Bake until the filling is set, about 25 to 30 minutes.
6. Take it out of the oven and allow it to cool fully.
7. After cooling, top with sliced almonds that have been toasted and dust with powdered sugar.
8. Cut into pieces and present.

Majorcan Almond Cake

Ingredients:

- 1 1/2 cups almond flour
- 1 cup granulated sugar
- 4 large eggs
- Zest of 1 lemon
- 1 teaspoon vanilla extract
- Powdered sugar (for dusting)

Instructions:

1. Set the oven's temperature to 175°C/350°F. Butter and dust a 9-inch circular cake pan.
2. Combine almond flour, granulated sugar, eggs, lemon zest, and vanilla essence in a sizable mixing basin and whisk until smooth.
3. Transfer the mixture to the ready-made cake pan.
4. Bake for 30 to 35 minutes, or until a toothpick inserted in the middle of the cake comes out clean and the cake is golden brown.
5. After the cake has cooled in the pan for ten minutes, move it to a wire rack to finish cooling.
6. Before serving, dust with powdered sugar. Cut and savour!

(Note: Traditional Gato Mallorquin does not contain any flour other than almond flour.**)**

Key Lime Tart with Graham Cracker Crust

Ingredients:

- 1 1/2 cups graham cracker crumbs
- 1/4 cup granulated sugar
- 6 tablespoons unsalted butter, melted
- 1 can (14 ounces) sweetened condensed milk
- 4 large egg yolks
- 1/2 cup key lime juice
- Zest of 1 lime
- Whipped cream (for serving)
- Lime slices (for garnish)

Instructions:

1. Set the oven's temperature to 175°C/350°F.
2. Place the melted butter, powdered sugar, and graham cracker crumbs in a mixing basin. Blend until thoroughly blended.
3. Fill a 9-inch tart pan with the mixture, pressing it up the sides and into the bottom.
4. After the crust has baked for ten minutes, take it out of the oven and allow it to cool.
5. Combine egg yolks, key lime juice, zest, and sweetened condensed milk in a different mixing bowl and whisk until smooth.
6. Fill the chilled crust with the filling.
7. Bake until the filling is set, about 15 to 20 minutes.
8. Before serving, let the tart cool fully and then place it in the refrigerator for at least two hours.
9. Top with slices of lime and serve with whipped cream.

Strawberry Shortcake with Fresh Whipped Cream

Ingredients:

- 2 cups all-purpose flour
- 1/4 cup granulated sugar
- 1 tablespoon baking powder
- 1/2 teaspoon salt
- 1/2 cup unsalted butter, cold and cubed
- 2/3 cup milk
- 1 teaspoon vanilla extract
- 2 cups sliced strawberries
- 1 tablespoon granulated sugar (for strawberries)
- Fresh whipped cream

Instructions:

1. Set the oven to 425°F (220°C). Line a baking sheet with parchment paper.
2. Combine the flour, sugar, baking powder, and salt in a sizable mixing bowl.
3. Using a pastry cutter or fork, chop in the chilled butter until the mixture resembles coarse crumbs.
4. Until just mixed, stir in milk and vanilla essence.
5. Place the dough on a surface dusted with flour and gently work it into a cohesive ball.
6. Using a biscuit cutter, pat the dough into a round that is one inch thick.
7. After the baking sheet is ready, place the dough circles on it and bake for 12 to 15 minutes or until golden brown.
8. Toss the sliced strawberries with 1 tablespoon of sugar and let them set for a few minutes while the shortcakes bake.
9. Horizontally split the cooled shortcakes in half. Top with whipped cream and strawberry slices. Cover the filling with the upper half of the shortcake.
10. Present right away and savour!

Raspberry Almond Tart with Shortcrust Pastry

Ingredients: For the shortcrust pastry:

- 1 1/2 cups all-purpose flour
- 1/2 cup unsalted butter, cold and cubed
- 1/4 cup granulated sugar
- 1 large egg yolk
- 2-3 tablespoons cold water

For the filling:

- 1 cup almond meal
- 1/2 cup granulated sugar
- 1/4 cup unsalted butter, melted
- 2 large eggs
- 1 teaspoon almond extract
- 1 cup fresh raspberries

Instructions:

1. Turn the oven on to 375°F, or 190°C.
2. Combine the flour, sugar, and butter in a food processor to make the shortcrust dough. Pulse the mixture until tiny breadcrumbs form.
3. Pulse the dough until it comes together after adding the egg yolk and the cold water. Take caution not to blend too much.
4. Using a floured surface, roll out the dough and line a 9-inch tart pan. Cut off any extra dough.
5. Blend almond meal, eggs, melted butter, granulated sugar, and almond essence in a mixing dish.
6. Using the prepared tart crust, evenly distribute the almond filling.
7. Top with a scattering of fresh raspberries and almond filling.
8. Bake for 25 to 30 minutes or until the crust is golden brown and the filling is set.
9. Allow the dessert to cool fully before cutting into slices and serving.

Red Velvet Cake with Cream Cheese Frosting

Ingredients: For the cake:

- 2 1/2 cups all-purpose flour
- 1 1/2 cups granulated sugar
- 1 teaspoon baking soda
- 1 teaspoon salt
- 1 teaspoon cocoa powder
- 1 1/2 cups vegetable oil
- 1 cup buttermilk, room temperature
- 2 large eggs, room temperature
- 2 tablespoons red food coloring
- 1 teaspoon white vinegar
- 1 teaspoon vanilla extract

For the cream cheese frosting:

- 16 ounces cream cheese, softened
- 1/2 cup unsalted butter, softened
- 4 cups powdered sugar
- 1 teaspoon vanilla extract

Instructions:

1. Set the oven's temperature to 175°C/350°F—butter and dust two 9-inch circular cake pans.
2. Combine the flour, sugar, baking soda, salt, and cocoa powder in a sizable mixing basin.
3. In a separate basin, thoroughly mix the vegetable oil, buttermilk, eggs, vinegar, red food colouring, and vanilla essence.

4. Add the wet components to the dry ones gradually and stir until smooth and thoroughly blended.
5. Divide the batter evenly among the cake pans that have been prepared.
6. Bake until a toothpick inserted into the centre comes out clean, 25 to 30 minutes.
7. After the cakes have cooled in the pans for ten minutes, move them to a wire rack to finish cooling.

Black Forest Cherry Cake with Kirsch-soaked Layers

Ingredients: For the cake layers:

- 1 3/4 cups all-purpose flour
- 3/4 cup unsweetened cocoa powder
- 1 1/2 teaspoons baking powder
- 1 1/2 teaspoons baking soda
- 1 teaspoon salt
- 2 cups granulated sugar
- 2 large eggs
- 1 cup milk
- 1/2 cup vegetable oil
- 2 teaspoons vanilla extract
- 1 cup boiling water

For the cherry filling:

- 2 cups pitted cherries, fresh or frozen
- 1/4 cup granulated sugar
- 1 tablespoon cornstarch
- 1 tablespoon lemon juice
- 2 tablespoons kirsch (cherry liqueur), optional

For the whipped cream frosting:

- 2 cups heavy cream, chilled
- 1/2 cup powdered sugar
- 1 teaspoon vanilla extract

For garnish:

- Additional pitted cherries
- Chocolate shavings

Instructions:

1. Set the oven's temperature to 175°C/350°F—butter and dust three 9-inch circular cake pans.
2. Combine flour, sugar, baking powder, baking soda, cocoa powder, and salt in a sizable mixing basin.
3. Mix the dry ingredients with the eggs, milk, oil, and vanilla essence. Beat for two minutes at a medium tempo.
4. Stir the batter thoroughly in the boiling water. There will be little batter.
5. Evenly divide the batter among cake pans that have been prepared.
6. Remove the toothpick from the centre after baking for 30 to 35 minutes.
7. After the cakes have cooled in the pans for ten minutes, move them to wire racks to finish cooling.

For the cherry filling:

1. Put the cherries, sugar, cornstarch, and lemon juice in a saucepan.
2. Cook, stirring regularly, over medium heat until the mixture thickens.

3. Turn off the heat and, if using, whisk in the kirsch. Before using, allow the filling to cool thoroughly.

For the whipped cream frosting:

1. Beat the heavy cream in a chilled mixing basin until soft peaks form.
2. Add vanilla extract and powdered sugar. Whipping should continue until stiff peaks develop.

Assembly:

1. Arrange one layer of cake onto a platter for serving. If desired, lightly dust the top with kirsch.
2. After putting whipped cream frosting on top of the cake layer, top the frosting with cherry filling.
3. Continue by adding the cherry filling, whipped cream icing, and remaining cake layers.
4. Use the leftover whipped cream frosting to decorate the cake's top and sides.
5. Add more cherries and chocolate shavings as garnish.
6. To allow the flavours to mingle together, chill the cake for at least an hour before serving.

CHAPTER - 6
CHEESE LOVER'S DELIGHT

Queso Fresco Empanadas

Ingredients:

- Queso fresco cheese
- Empanada dough (store-bought or homemade)
- Egg wash (1 egg beaten with a tablespoon of water)

Instructions:

1. Roll out the dough for the empanadas and cut into circles.
2. In the centre of each circle, place a tiny slice of queso fresco cheese.
3. Fold the dough over the cheese, then use a fork to press the edges together.
4. Use egg wash to brush the empanadas.
5. Bake for 20 to 25 minutes, or until golden brown, in an oven that has been set to 375°F (190°C).

Manchego Cheese Bread Rolls

Ingredients:

- Bread dough (store-bought or homemade)
- Manchego cheese, grated

Instructions:

1. Create a rectangle shape out of the bread dough.
2. Evenly distribute grated Manchego cheese throughout the dough.
3. Tightly roll the dough, then cut it into slices.

4. After placing the slices on a baking pan, give them 30 minutes to rise.
5. Bake for 25 to 30 minutes or until golden brown in an oven that has been set to 350°F (175°C).

Spanish Cheese Stuffed Peppers

Ingredients:

- Bell peppers
- Spanish cheese blend (e.g., Manchego, Mahón, Idiazabal)
- Olive oil
- Salt and pepper to taste

Instructions:

1. Cut off the bell peppers' tops and take out the seeds.
2. Stuff the Spanish cheese mixture inside each pepper.
3. Add a drizzle of olive oil and season with pepper and salt.
4. Arrange the peppers on a baking sheet and bake for 25 to 30 minutes, or until the cheese is melted and bubbling, at 375°F (190°C) in a preheated oven.

Tortilla Espanola with Queso Blanco

Ingredients:

- Potatoes, thinly sliced
- Eggs
- Queso Blanco cheese, diced
- Onion, thinly sliced
- Olive oil
- Salt and pepper to taste

Instructions:

1. Add the onions and potatoes, thinly sliced, to a skillet with heated olive oil. Simmer the potatoes until they become soft.
2. Beat the eggs in a bowl and add pepper and salt to taste.
3. Thoroughly combine the beaten eggs with the cooked potatoes, onions, and diced queso blanco cheese.
4. Return the mixture to the skillet and heat it there over medium heat until the edges begin to firm up.
5. Cover the skillet with a plate, then flip the tortilla onto it.
6. Return the tortilla to the skillet and cook it until it is golden brown on both sides and the eggs are set.

Serrano Ham and Manchego Cheese Pinwheels

Ingredients:

- Puff pastry dough
- Manchego cheese, grated
- Serrano ham slices

Instructions:

1. Using the puff pastry dough, roll it out into a rectangle.
2. Evenly distribute grated Manchego cheese throughout the dough.
3. Arrange slices of Serrano ham over the cheese.
4. Tightly roll the dough and cut it into pinwheels.
5. Arrange the pinwheels on a baking sheet and bake for 15 to 20 minutes or until golden brown and crispy, at 375°F (190°C) in a preheated oven.

Cheese and Chorizo Empanadillas

Ingredients:

- Empanada dough (store-bought or homemade)
- Chorizo sausage, diced
- Spanish cheese blend (e.g., Manchego, Mahón, Idiazabal), grated

Instructions:

1. Roll out the dough for the empanadas and cut into circles.
2. Top each circle with a dollop of grated Spanish cheese and sliced chorizo.
3. Fold the dough over the filling, then use a fork to press the sides together.
4. Transfer the empanadillas to a baking sheet and bake for 20 to 25 minutes, or until golden brown, at 375°F (190°C) in a preheated oven.

Basque Cheesecake with Quince Paste

Ingredients:

- Cream cheese
- Eggs
- Sugar
- Flour
- Quince paste (membrillo)

Instructions:

1. Set the oven's temperature to 400°F or 200°C.
2. Using a bowl, thoroughly combine the cream cheese, eggs, sugar, and flour.
3. Spoon the mixture into a cake pan that has been buttered.

4. Place a dollop of quince paste over the cheesecake mixture.
5. Bake the cheesecake for 40 to 45 minutes or until the top is golden brown and firm.
6. Before slicing and serving, let it cool.

Spanish Cheese and Spinach Puff Pastry Triangles

Ingredients:

- Puff pastry dough
- Spanish cheese blend (e.g., Manchego, Mahon, Idiazabal), grated
- Spinach, cooked and chopped

Instructions:

1. The puff pastry dough should be rolled out and cut into triangles.
2. In a bowl, combine cooked, chopped spinach and grated Spanish cheese.
3. Top each triangle with a dollop of the cheese and spinach mixture.
4. To create triangles, fold the dough over the filling and bind the edges.
5. Arrange the triangles on a baking sheet and bake for 15 to 20 minutes, or until golden brown, at 375°F (190°C) in a preheated oven.

Galician Cheese and Potato Pie

Ingredients:

- Potatoes, thinly sliced
- Spanish cheese blend (e.g., Tetilla, San Simon, Arzua-Ulloa), grated
- Eggs
- Milk
- Salt and pepper to taste

Instructions:

1. Turn the oven on to 375°F, or 190°C.
2. Arrange the potatoes in a baking dish that has been oiled with oil.
3. Top the potatoes with a grating combination of Spanish cheese.
4. Whisk the eggs, milk, salt, and pepper in another basin.
5. Cover the potatoes and cheese with the egg mixture.
6. Bake for 30 to 35 minutes, or until the tops of the eggs are golden brown and the eggs are set.

Mahon Cheese Fritters with Honey Drizzle

Ingredients:

- Mahon cheese, cubed
- Flour
- Baking powder
- Eggs
- Milk
- Honey for drizzling

Instructions:

1. Combine the flour and baking powder in a bowl.
2. Beat the eggs and milk together in another basin.
3. Coat the Mahon cheese cubes with the flour mixture after dipping them into the egg mixture.
4. Until golden brown, deep fried the coated cheese cubes.
5. Before serving, drizzle some honey over.

Cheese and Olive Breadsticks

Ingredients:

- Breadstick dough (store-bought or homemade)
- Spanish cheese blend (e.g., Manchego, Mahón, Idiazabal), grated
- Pitted green olives, chopped

Instructions:

1. Use the breadstick dough to roll it out into thin strips.
2. Top each strip with a little bit of chopped olives and grated Spanish cheese.
3. Place the strips on a baking sheet after twisting them.
4. Bake for 12 to 15 minutes, or until golden brown, in an oven that has been set to 375°F (190°C).

Catalan Cheese and Tomato Flatbread

Ingredients:

- Pizza dough
- Manchego cheese, grated
- Cherry tomatoes, halved
- Olive oil
- Fresh basil leaves

- Salt and pepper to taste

Instructions:

1. Use the pizza dough to roll it out into a rectangle.
2. Top the dough with grated Manchego cheese.
3. Place the cherry tomatoes, cut in half, on top.
4. Add a drizzle of olive oil and season with pepper and salt.
5. Bake for fifteen to twenty minutes, or until the crust is golden brown, at 425°F (220°C) in a preheated oven.
6. Before serving, garnish with fresh basil leaves.

Spanish Cheese and Herb Scones

Ingredients:

- All-purpose flour
- Baking powder
- Salt
- Butter
- Spanish cheese blend (e.g., Manchego, Mahon, Idiazabal), grated
- Fresh herbs (such as thyme, rosemary, or oregano), chopped
- Milk

Instructions:

1. Set the oven's temperature to 425°F (220°C).
2. Combine the flour, baking powder, and salt in a bowl.
3. Until the mixture resembles coarse crumbs, cut in butter.
4. Add chopped fresh herbs and grated Spanish cheese.
5. Stirring constantly, and gradually add milk until a soft dough forms.
6. Spoon dough onto a baking sheet in spoonfuls.

7. Bake for a beautiful brown colour, 12 to 15 minutes.

Arroz con Queso (Spanish Rice with Cheese)

Ingredients:

- Long-grain rice
- Chicken broth
- Onion, finely chopped
- Garlic, minced
- Spanish cheese blend (e.g., Manchego, Mahon, Idiazabal), grated
- Olive oil
- Salt and pepper to taste

Instructions:

1. Heat the olive oil in a pot and sauté the onion and garlic until they become tender.
2. Cook the rice for a few minutes or until it starts to toast slightly.
3. Add the chicken broth and heat it until it boils.
4. After the rice is cooked and the liquid has been absorbed, lower the heat, cover, and simmer.
5. Mix in the grated Spanish cheese until it melts and blends thoroughly.
6. Before serving, season with salt and pepper.

Cheese-Stuffed Mushrooms a la Española

Ingredients:

- Giant mushrooms, cleaned and stems removed
- Spanish cheese blend (e.g., Manchego, Mahon, Idiazabal), grated
- Garlic, minced
- Olive oil
- Fresh parsley, chopped
- Salt and pepper to taste

Instructions:

1. Turn the oven on to 375°F, or 190°C.
2. Combine grated Spanish cheese, parsley, minced garlic, olive oil, salt, and pepper in a bowl.
3. Stuff the cheese mixture into each mushroom cap.
4. Arrange the filled mushrooms onto an oven tray.
5. Bake for 15 to 20 minutes, or until the cheese is bubbling and melted and the mushrooms are soft.
6. Garnish with more chopped parsley, if desired, and serve hot.

CHAPTER - 7

SPANISH BREAD ROLLS AND BUNS RECIPES

Pan de Leche (Milk Bread Rolls)

Ingredients:

- 500g bread flour
- 10g instant yeast
- 250ml warm milk
- 50g sugar
- 50g butter
- 1 tsp salt

Instructions:

1. Combine warm milk, sugar, and yeast in a bowl. Wait five minutes for it to get frothy.
2. Include the butter, flour, and salt in the yeast mixture. Work the dough until it becomes smooth.
3. After it has doubled in size, cover it and let it rise for about an hour.
4. Form the dough into rolls by dividing it into equal sections.
5. Transfer to a baking sheet, cover, and allow to rise for an additional half-hour.
6. Set oven temperature to 350°F/180°C. Cook for 20 to 25 minutes or until well browned.

Bollos de Aceite (Olive Oil Buns)

Ingredients:

- 400g bread flour
- 10g instant yeast
- 250ml warm water
- 50ml olive oil
- 1 tsp salt
- 1 tbsp sugar

Instructions:

1. Combine warm water, sugar, and yeast in a bowl. Let it froth for five minutes.
2. To the yeast mixture, add salt, flour, and olive oil. Work until smooth.
3. After it has doubled in size, cover it and let it rise for about an hour.
4. Form the dough into buns by dividing it into equal sections.
5. Transfer to a baking sheet, cover, and allow to rise for an additional half-hour.
6. Set the oven temperature to 200°C (400°F)—coat in the oven for 15 to 20 minutes until browned.

Cadiz Bread Rolls

Ingredients:

- 450g bread flour
- 10g instant yeast
- 250ml warm water
- 1 tsp salt
- 1 tbsp honey

Instructions:

1. In warm water, dissolve the yeast and honey. Until foamy, let it sit for five minutes.
2. In a bowl, combine flour and salt. Knead until smooth after adding the yeast mixture.
3. After it has doubled in size, cover it and let it rise for about an hour.
4. Form the dough into rolls by dividing it into equal sections.
5. Transfer to a baking sheet, cover, and allow to rise for an additional half-hour.
6. Set oven temperature to 190°C (375°F). Bake for 20–25 minutes or until just starting to brown.

Spanish Potato Bread Rolls

Ingredients:

- 350g bread flour
- 150g mashed potatoes
- 10g instant yeast
- 200ml warm milk
- 50g butter
- 1 tsp salt

Instructions:

1. Combine yeast, warm milk, and mashed potatoes. Wait five minutes for it to get frothy.
2. Include the butter, flour, and salt in the potato mixture. Work until smooth.
3. After it has doubled in size, cover it and let it rise for about an hour.

4. Form the dough into rolls by dividing it into equal sections.
5. Transfer to a baking sheet, cover, and allow to rise for an additional half-hour.
6. Set oven temperature to 350°F/180°C. Cook for 20 to 25 minutes or until well browned.

Pan de Maiz (Cornbread Rolls)

Ingredients:

- 300g cornmeal
- 200g bread flour
- 10g instant yeast
- 250ml warm water
- 50g butter
- 1 tsp salt
- 1 tbsp honey

Instructions:

1. In a bowl, combine cornmeal, bread flour, yeast, and salt.
2. Stir in melted butter, honey, and warm water. Work until smooth.
3. After it has doubled in size, cover it and let it rise for about an hour.
4. Form the dough into rolls by dividing it into equal sections.
5. Transfer to a baking sheet, cover, and allow to rise for an additional half-hour.
6. Set the oven temperature to 200°C (400°F)—coat in the oven for 15 to 20 minutes until browned.

Pan de Queso (Spanish Cheese Bread Rolls)

Ingredients:

- 400g bread flour
- 10g instant yeast
- 250ml warm milk
- 100g grated cheese (such as Manchego or Cheddar)
- 50g butter
- 1 tsp salt

Instructions:

1. Mix warm milk with yeast. Until foamy, let it sit for five minutes.
2. In a bowl, combine flour, salt, melted butter, and grated cheese. Knead until smooth after adding the yeast mixture.
3. After it has doubled in size, cover it and let it rise for about an hour.
4. Form the dough into rolls by dividing it into equal sections.
5. Transfer to a baking sheet, cover, and allow to rise for an additional half-hour.
6. Set oven temperature to 350°F/180°C. Cook for 20 to 25 minutes or until well browned.

Spanish Anise Bread Rolls

Ingredients:

- 500g bread flour
- 10g instant yeast
- 250ml warm water

- 50g sugar
- 50ml olive oil
- 1 tsp salt
- 1 tbsp anise seeds

Instructions:

1. Dissolve the yeast and sugar in the heated water. Until foamy, let it sit for five minutes.
2. In a bowl, combine flour, salt, and anise seeds. Stir in the yeast mixture and olive oil. Work until smooth.
3. After it has doubled in size, cover it and let it rise for about an hour.
4. Form the dough into rolls by dividing it into equal sections.
5. Transfer to a baking sheet, cover, and allow to rise for an additional half-hour.
6. Set oven temperature to 190°C (375°F). Bake for 20–25 minutes or until just starting to brown.

Antequera Bread Rolls

Ingredients:

- 450g bread flour
- 10g instant yeast
- 250ml warm milk
- 50g sugar
- 50g lard or shortening
- 1 tsp salt

Instructions:

1. Mix warm milk with sugar and yeast. Until foamy, let it sit for five minutes.

2. In a bowl, combine flour, salt, and lard. Knead until smooth after adding the yeast mixture.
3. After it has doubled in size, cover it and let it rise for about an hour.
4. Form the dough into rolls by dividing it into equal sections.
5. Transfer to a baking sheet, cover, and allow to rise for an additional half-hour.
6. Set oven temperature to 350°F/180°C. Cook for 20 to 25 minutes or until well browned.

Calatrava Bread Rolls

Ingredients:

- 400g bread flour
- 10g instant yeast
- 250ml warm water
- 1 tsp salt
- 1 tbsp honey
- 50g raisins

Instructions:

1. In warm water, dissolve the yeast and honey. Until foamy, let it sit for five minutes.
2. In a bowl, combine flour, salt, and raisins. Knead until smooth after adding the yeast mixture.
3. After it has doubled in size, cover it and let it rise for about an hour.
4. Form the dough into rolls by dividing it into equal sections.
5. Transfer to a baking sheet, cover, and allow to rise for an additional half-hour.

6. Set oven temperature to 190°C (375°F). Bake for 20–25 minutes or until just starting to brown.

Spanish Sobrasada Sausage Buns

Ingredients:

- 400g bread flour
- 10g instant yeast
- 250ml warm milk
- 100g sobrasada sausage
- 50g grated cheese (such as Manchego)
- 1 tsp salt

Instructions:

1. Mix warm milk with yeast. Until foamy, let it sit for five minutes.
2. In a bowl, combine flour and salt. Add the shredded cheese, sobrasada sausage, and yeast mixture. Work until smooth.
3. After it has doubled in size, cover it and let it rise for about an hour.
4. Form the dough into buns by dividing it into equal sections.
5. Transfer to a baking sheet, cover, and allow to rise for an additional half-hour.
6. Set oven temperature to 350°F/180°C. Cook for 20 to 25 minutes or until well browned.

Spanish Wine Rolls

Ingredients:

- 450g bread flour
- 10g instant yeast
- 250ml red wine
- 50g sugar
- 50ml olive oil
- 1 tsp salt

Instructions:

1. Use red wine to dissolve yeast and sugar. Until foamy, let it sit for five minutes.
2. Combine flour, salt, and olive oil in a bowl. Knead in the wine mixture until smooth.
3. After it has doubled in size, cover it and let it rise for about an hour.
4. Form the dough into rolls by dividing it into equal sections.
5. Transfer to a baking sheet, cover, and allow to rise for an additional half-hour.
6. Set oven temperature to 190°C (375°F). Bake for 20–25 minutes or until just starting to brown.

Spanish Olive Bread Rolls

Ingredients:

- 400g bread flour
- 10g instant yeast
- 250ml warm water
- 100g chopped olives
- 50ml olive oil

- 1 tsp salt

Instructions:

1. Dissolve the yeast in a warm solution. Until foamy, let it sit for five minutes.
2. In a bowl, combine flour, salt, olive oil, and chopped olives. Knead until smooth after adding the yeast mixture.
3. After it has doubled in size, cover it and let it rise for about an hour.
4. Form the dough into rolls by dividing it into equal sections.
5. Transfer to a baking sheet, cover, and allow to rise for an additional half-hour.
6. Set oven temperature to 350°F/180°C. Cook for 20 to 25 minutes or until well browned.

Spanish Spelt Bread Rolls

Ingredients:

- 400g spelt flour
- 10g instant yeast
- 250ml warm water
- 50g honey
- 50ml olive oil
- 1 tsp salt

Instructions:

1. In warm water, dissolve the yeast and honey. Until foamy, let it sit for five minutes.
2. In a bowl, combine spelt flour, salt, and olive oil. Knead until smooth after adding the yeast mixture.

3. After it has doubled in size, cover it and let it rise for about an hour.
4. Form the dough into rolls by dividing it into equal sections.
5. Transfer to a baking sheet, cover, and allow to rise for an additional half-hour.
6. Set oven temperature to 350°F/180°C. Cook for 20 to 25 minutes or until well browned.

Spanish Chocolate Buns

Ingredients:

- 350g bread flour
- 50g cocoa powder
- 10g instant yeast
- 250ml warm milk
- 50g sugar
- 50g butter
- 1 tsp salt

Instructions:

1. Mix warm milk with sugar and yeast. Until foamy, let it sit for five minutes.
2. In a bowl, combine bread flour, melted butter, cocoa powder, and salt. Knead until smooth after adding the yeast mixture.
3. After it has doubled in size, cover it and let it rise for about an hour.
4. Form the dough into rolls by dividing it into equal sections.
5. Transfer to a baking sheet, cover, and allow to rise for an additional half-hour.

6. Set oven temperature to 350°F/180°C. Cook for 20 to 25 minutes or until well browned.

Spanish Fig Bread Rolls

Ingredients:

- 400g bread flour
- 10g instant yeast
- 250ml warm water
- 100g dried figs, chopped
- 50g honey
- 1 tsp salt

Instructions:

1. In warm water, dissolve the yeast and honey. Until foamy, let it sit for five minutes.
2. In a basin, combine bread flour, salt, and chopped dried figs. Knead until smooth after adding the yeast mixture.
3. After it has doubled in size, cover it and let it rise for about an hour.
4. Form the dough into rolls by dividing it into equal sections.
5. Transfer to a baking sheet, cover, and allow to rise for an additional half-hour.
6. Set oven temperature to 350°F/180°C. Cook for 20 to 25 minutes or until well browned.

CHAPTER - 8

AFTERNOON TEA-TIME TREATS FROM SPAIN RECIPES

Churros con Chocolate

Ingredients:

- 1 cup water
- 2 1/2 tablespoons white sugar
- 1/2 teaspoon salt
- 2 tablespoons vegetable oil
- 1 cup all-purpose flour
- 2 quarts oil for frying
- 1/2 cup white sugar, or to taste
- 1 teaspoon ground cinnamon

Instructions:

1. Heat 2 1/2 tablespoons sugar, 2 tablespoons vegetable oil, and water in a small skillet over medium heat. After bringing to a boil, turn off the heat. Add flour and stir until a ball of mixture forms.
2. Preheat the oil in a deep fryer or skillet to 375 degrees Fahrenheit or 190 degrees Celsius. I am using a pastry bag and pipe dough strips into the heated oil. When golden, fry them and then drain on paper towels.
3. Mix cinnamon and 1/2 cup sugar. Dredge the drained churros in a combination of sugar and cinnamon.

Spanish Lemon Muffins

Ingredients:

- 2 eggs
- 1/2 cup white sugar
- 1/2 cup milk
- 1/2 cup vegetable oil
- 1 1/2 cups all-purpose flour
- 1 teaspoon baking powder
- Zest of 1 lemon

Instructions:

1. Turn the oven on to 350 degrees Fahrenheit (175 degrees Celsius). Use paper muffin liners or grease the muffin tins.
2. Beat eggs and sugar in a medium-sized bowl until light and fluffy. Add oil and milk, and stir. Mix baking powder and flour, then gently add them to the egg mixture. Stir in the lemon zest. Pour the batter into muffin tins to two-thirds full.
3. In a preheated oven, bake for 20 to 25 minutes or until a toothpick inserted into the centre of a muffin comes out clean.

Fruit Turnovers

Ingredients:

- 2 cups all-purpose flour
- 1/4 teaspoon salt
- 2/3 cup shortening
- 5 tablespoons cold water
- Fruit filling of your choice (e.g., apples, peaches, strawberries)

- 1/4 cup white sugar
- 1/2 teaspoon ground cinnamon

Instructions:

1. Set oven temperature to 375 F, or 190 C.
2. Mix the flour and salt in a big bowl. Cut in the shortening until the mixture resembles coarse crumbs. Add water and stir until a ball of mixture forms.
3. Roll out the dough to a thickness of 1/8 inch on a surface dusted with flour. Cut into rounds that are 6 inches in diameter.
4. Top each circular with a teaspoon of fruit filling. Enclose the filling with dough, pressing the edges together to seal. Arrange the turnovers onto a baking tray.
5. Mix the sugar and cinnamon in a small bowl. Sprinkle on top of turnovers.
6. Bake for 20 to 25 minutes, or until golden brown, in a preheated oven.

Spanish Palmiers

Ingredients:

- 1 sheet puff pastry, thawed
- 1/2 cup granulated sugar

Instructions:

1. Set the oven's temperature to 400°F or 200°C. Use parchment paper to line a baking sheet.
2. Use half of the sugar to sprinkle half of a clean work surface. On top of the sugar, unfold the puff pastry sheet. Evenly distribute the leftover sugar on top of the puff pastry.

3. Gently roll the puff pastry into a rectangle with a rolling pin, pressing the sugar into the dough.
4. Fold the puff pastry's borders toward the centre, meeting in the middle, starting from the long sides. To form a log, fold the dough again down the centerline.
5. Using a sharp knife, cut the log into pieces that are 1/2 inch thick. With the cut side down, arrange the slices on the prepared baking sheet, allowing space between each palmier.
6. Bake the palmiers for 12 to 15 minutes, or until they are crispy and golden brown, in a preheated oven.
7. After a few minutes of cooling on the baking sheet, move the palmiers to a wire rack to finish cooling.

Orange Cake

Ingredients:

- 4 eggs
- 1 cup white sugar
- 1/2 cup vegetable oil
- 1/2 cup orange juice
- 1 tablespoon orange zest
- 1 1/2 cups all-purpose flour
- 2 teaspoons baking powder
- Powdered sugar for dusting (optional)

Instructions:

1. Set oven temperature to 175°C/350°F. Butter and dust a 9-inch circular cake pan.
2. Beat eggs and sugar together in a sizable mixing bowl until light and frothy.

3. Until wholly blended, stir in vegetable oil, orange juice, and orange zest.
4. Sift the flour and baking powder together in another basin. Mixing until smooth, gradually incorporate the dry ingredients into the wet ones.
5. Fill the cake pan with the batter.
6. Bake for 30 to 35 minutes, or until a toothpick inserted in the centre comes out clean, in a preheated oven.
7. After the cake has cooled in the pan for ten minutes, move it to a wire rack to finish cooling.
8. If preferred, sprinkle with powdered sugar prior to serving.

Spanish Pastry Crescents

Ingredients:

- 2 cups all-purpose flour
- 1/2 cup granulated sugar
- 1/2 teaspoon baking powder
- 1/2 cup unsalted butter, cold and diced
- 1 large egg
- 1 tablespoon milk
- 1/2 cup fruit jam or filling of your choice (e.g., apricot, raspberry)
- Powdered sugar for dusting (optional)

Instructions:

1. Set oven temperature to 175°C/350°F. Use parchment paper to line a baking sheet.
2. Combine the flour, sugar, and baking powder in a sizable bowl.

3. Using your hands, work the cold, chopped butter into the flour mixture until the mixture resembles coarse breadcrumbs.
4. Beat together the egg and milk in a small bowl. Stirring constantly, gradually incorporate the egg mixture into the flour mixture until the dough comes together.
5. Place the dough on a lightly floured surface and slowly work it into a smooth texture. Roll out the dough to a thickness of about 1/4 inch.
6. Cut dough into rounds using a glass or round cookie cutter. Put one spoonful of filling or fruit jam in the middle of each round.
7. Press the edges of the folded circles together to create crescent shapes.
8. Transfer the pastis sets to the prepared baking sheet and bake for 12 to 15 minutes, or until they begin to turn a light golden colour.
9. After a few minutes of cooling on the baking sheet, move the pastissets to a wire rack to finish cooling.
10. If preferred, sprinkle with powdered sugar prior to serving.

Spanish Wind Fritters

Ingredients:

- 1 cup water
- 1/2 cup unsalted butter
- 1 cup all-purpose flour
- 4 eggs
- Zest of 1 lemon
- Vegetable oil for frying
- Powdered sugar for dusting

Instructions:

1. Boil the butter and water in a pot. Once the mixture comes together into a ball, stir in the flour and lemon zest.
2. Pour the mixture into a mixing bowl and let it cool a bit. Beat in one egg at a time until smooth.
3. Preheat a big pot or deep fryer to 375°F (190°C) using vegetable oil.
4. Drop heaping spoonfuls of dough into the heated oil and cook for two to three minutes on each side or until golden brown.
5. Take the cakes out of the oil and place them on paper towels to drain.
6. Before serving, dust the bunuelos with powdered sugar. It's best to eat them warm.

Spanish Olive Oil Biscuits

Ingredients:

- 2 cups all-purpose flour
- 1/2 teaspoon baking powder
- 1/4 teaspoon salt
- 1/4 cup extra virgin olive oil
- 1/4 cup water
- 1/4 cup white wine
- 1 teaspoon anise seeds (optional)
- 1 tablespoon granulated sugar

Instructions:

1. Preheat the oven to 375°F (190°C) and place parchment paper on a baking pan.
2. Combine the flour, baking powder, salt, and anise seeds (if using) in a sizable bowl.

3. Combine the white wine, water, and olive oil in another bowl.
4. Stirring constantly, gradually combine the wet and dry ingredients to make a dough.
5. Form the dough into thin circles by dividing it into tiny sections.
6. Transfer the dough circles to the baking sheet that has been prepared, then lightly dust each one with powdered sugar.
7. Bake for 12 to 15 minutes, or until crispy and golden brown, in a preheated oven.
8. Before serving, let the tortas de aceite cool on the baking pan. When paired with tea or coffee, they taste great.

Spanish French Toast

Ingredients:

- 1 loaf of day-old bread (preferably a dense bread like brioche or baguette), sliced into thick pieces
- 2 cups whole milk
- 1 cinnamon stick
- Zest of 1 lemon
- 4 eggs
- 1/2 cup granulated sugar
- Olive oil or butter for frying
- Ground cinnamon for dusting

Instructions:

1. Simmer the milk in a pot with the lemon zest and cinnamon stick. Take it off the fire and let it cool a little.
2. Beat the eggs and sugar together thoroughly on a small plate.

3. Soak the bread slices in the warm milk mixture for a few minutes to ensure they are thoroughly coated.
4. In a skillet over medium heat, preheat butter or olive oil.
5. Fry the drenched bread pieces for two to three minutes on each side or until golden brown.
6. To get rid of extra oil, take the torrijas out of the skillet and drain them on paper towels.
7. Sprinkle some ground cinnamon over the torrijas and serve them hot. If preferred, they can also be served with a drizzle of maple syrup or honey.

Spanish Almond Cookies

Ingredients:

- 2 cups almond flour
- 1 cup granulated sugar
- Zest of 1 lemon
- 2 egg yolks
- 1/4 cup pine nuts or chopped almonds (for coating)

Instructions:

1. Preheat the oven to 350°F (180°C) and place parchment paper on a baking pan.
2. Place the sugar, lemon zest, and almond flour in a mixing bowl.
3. Stir the dry ingredients and egg yolks together until a dough forms.
4. Pinch out little dough pieces and form them into balls with a diameter of approximately an inch.
5. To coat each ball, roll it in chopped almonds or pine nuts.
6. Transfer the coated balls to the prepared baking sheet and gently flatten them with your fingers.

7. Bake for 12 to 15 minutes, or until the cookies are golden brown, in an oven that has been warmed.
8. Let the pellets cool for a few minutes on the baking sheet, then move them to a wire rack to finish cooling.

Spanish Pork Crackling Flatbread

Ingredients:

- 2 cups all-purpose flour
- 1 teaspoon salt
- 1/2 cup olive oil
- 1/2 cup water
- 1 cup pork cracklings (lardons)
- Sea salt for sprinkling

Instructions:

1. Preheat the oven to 400°F (200°C), and place parchment paper on a baking pan.
2. Combine the flour and salt in a mixing bowl. Gradually add the water and olive oil while mixing until a dough forms.
3. Using a lightly floured surface, knead the dough until it becomes elastic and smooth.
4. Split the dough into two equal pieces, then roll out each to form a slender rectangle on the baking sheet that has been ready.
5. Evenly distribute and gently press the pork cracklings into the dough rectangles.
6. Lightly dust the dough with sea salt.
7. In a preheated oven, bake for 20 to 25 minutes or until the flatbread is crispy and golden brown.

8. Before slicing and serving, remove the cake from the oven and allow it to cool slightly. Savour the flavorful and crunchy coca de lardons!

Spanish Custard

Ingredients:

- 4 cups whole milk
- 1 cinnamon stick
- Zest of 1 lemon
- 6 egg yolks
- 1 cup granulated sugar
- 1/4 cup cornstarch
- 1 teaspoon vanilla extract
- Brown sugar (for caramelizing)

Instructions:

1. Simmer the milk in a pot with the lemon zest and cinnamon stick. Take it off the burner and give it ten minutes to infuse. Take out the lemon zest and cinnamon stick.
2. Combine the egg yolks, sugar, and cornstarch in a bowl and whisk until smooth.
3. Whisk continuously as you gradually add the heated milk to the egg mixture.
4. Transfer the mixture back to the saucepan and stir continuously over medium heat until it thickens to the point where a spoon can easily slide through it.
5. Turn off the heat source and mix in the vanilla essence.
6. Transfer the custard into individual ramekins and chill for a minimum of two hours or until it solidifies.

7. Before serving, use a cooking torch or broiler to caramelize a thin coating of brown sugar on top of each custard.

Spanish Sweet Spiral Buns

Ingredients:

- 4 cups all-purpose flour
- 1/2 cup warm milk
- 1/4 cup granulated sugar
- 2 teaspoons active dry yeast
- 4 large eggs
- 1/2 cup unsalted butter, softened
- Powdered sugar for dusting

Instructions:

1. In a small basin, dissolve the yeast and a small amount of sugar in warm milk. Let it sit until frothy for five to ten minutes.
2. Place the flour, eggs, softened butter, and remaining sugar in a large mixing bowl and blend thoroughly.
3. Combine the yeast mixture with the flour mixture and knead the dough until it becomes elastic and smooth.
4. Tightly cover the dough with a fresh towel and allow it to rise in a warm location until it has doubled in size, around one to two hours.
5. Flatten the dough and separate it into equal pieces.
6. Create a thin rectangle out of each part, then coil it up into a spiral.
7. Arrange the formed buns, with space between them, on a baking sheet covered with parchment paper.
8. Give the buns another 30 to 45 minutes to rise.

9. Set oven temperature to 180°C or 350°F.
10. Bake for 15 to 20 minutes or until golden brown on the buns.
11. Take them out of the oven and give them a little time to cool down before sprinkling with powdered sugar.

Spanish Apple Tart

Ingredients:

- 1 sheet of puff pastry, thawed
- 4-5 apples, peeled, cored, and thinly sliced
- 1/4 cup granulated sugar
- 1 teaspoon ground cinnamon
- 2 tablespoons unsalted butter, cut into small pieces
- Apricot jam (for glazing)

Instructions:

1. Turn the oven on to 375°F, or 190°C.
2. Using a surface dusted with flour, roll out the puff pastry and place it on a baking sheet lined with parchment.
3. Leaving a border around the borders, arrange the apple slices in an overlapping pattern on top of the puff pastry.
4. Combine the sugar and cinnamon in a small bowl. Evenly distribute the mixture over the apples.
5. Use small bits of butter to adorn the tops of the apples.
6. Bake the tart for 25 to 30 minutes, or until the apples are soft and the dough is golden brown, in a preheated oven.
7. In a small saucepan, bring the apricot jam to a boil. Brush the warmed tart with the melted jam for a glossy finish.
8. Let the tart cool a little before cutting into slices and serving. Have fun!

Torta de Aceite (Spanish Olive Oil Flatbread)

Ingredients:

- All-purpose flour
- Olive oil
- Salt
- Water

Instructions:

1. Combine flour, salt, and olive oil in a mixing basin.
2. Add water gradually while mixing to produce a smooth dough.
3. Shape the dough into flatbreads by dividing it into balls.
4. Cook the flatbreads in a pan over medium heat until they are golden brown on both sides.

Spanish Spelt Bread

Ingredients:

- Spelt flour
- Yeast
- Water
- Salt

Instructions:

1. Let the yeast dissolve in the warm water and leave it for five minutes.

2. Combine the yeast mixture, spelt flour, and salt in a mixing dish.
3. Work the dough into an elastic and smooth texture.
4. After the dough has doubled in size, put it in an oiled loaf pan, cover it, and let it rise.
5. Bake for 30 to 35 minutes, or until golden brown, in an oven that has been set to 375°F (190°C).

Spanish Almond Ring Cookies

Ingredients:

- Almond flour
- Sugar
- Egg whites
- Almond extract

Instructions:

1. Preheat the oven to 350°F (175°C), and place parchment paper on a baking pan.
2. Gently stir together almond flour, sugar, egg whites, and almond extract in a bowl.
3. Shape the dough into rings, then arrange them on the ready baking sheet.
4. Bake until golden brown, 12 to 15 minutes.

Spanish Corn Empanadas

Ingredients:

- Corn flour
- Water
- Salt

- Fillings of your choice (such as cheese, vegetables, or meat)

Instructions:

1. Combine corn flour and salt in a bowl.
2. While kneading, gradually add water until a smooth dough develops.
3. Using your hands, spread out each small ball of dough into a thin circle.
4. Fill each circle to the brim with a spoonful of filling, fold over, and seal the edges.
5. Bake or fry the empanadillas until crispy and golden brown.

Torta de Almendra y Naranja (Almond and Orange Cake)

Ingredients:

- Almond flour
- Orange zest
- Sugar
- Eggs
- Baking powder

Instructions:

1. Preheat the oven to 350°F (175°C), and coat a cake pan with oil.
2. Using an electric mixer, thoroughly blend almond flour, sugar, orange zest, eggs, and baking powder in a mixing dish.

3. Transfer the mixture to the prepared pan and bake it for thirty to thirty-five minutes, or until a toothpick inserted into the centre comes out clean.
4. Before serving, allow the cake to cool.

Spanish Rye Bread

Ingredients:

- Rye flour
- Yeast
- Water
- Salt

Instructions:

1. Let the yeast dissolve in the warm water and leave it for five minutes.
2. Combine the yeast mixture, rye flour, and salt in a mixing dish.
3. Work the dough into an elastic and smooth texture.
4. Form the dough into a loaf, put it in a greased loaf pan, cover it, and allow it to rise until it doubles in size.
5. Bake for 40 to 45 minutes, or until the bread sounds hollow when tapped on the bottom, in an oven that has been set to 375°F (190°C).

Tortitas de Patata (Potato Pancakes)

Ingredients:

- Potatoes
- Onion
- Eggs
- Flour

- Salt
- Olive oil

Instructions:

1. After grating the potatoes and onion, remove any extra moisture.
2. To make a batter, combine the grated potatoes, onion, eggs, flour, and salt in a bowl.
3. In a frying pan, warm the olive oil over medium heat.
4. Using a spatula, flatten parts of the batter after dropping them into the heated oil.
5. Cook until both sides are golden brown. Before serving, drain on paper towels.

Spanish Oat Muffins

Ingredients:

- Oat flour
- Sugar
- Eggs
- Milk
- Baking powder
- Olive oil

Instructions:

1. Adjust the oven temperature to 350°F (175°C) and place paper liners into a muffin tray.
2. Combine the oat flour, sugar, eggs, milk, baking powder, and olive oil in a bowl and mix until well combined.
3. Fill each of the muffin tin cups to about two-thirds full with the batter.

4. Bake until a toothpick inserted into the centre comes out clean, about 15 to 20 minutes.
5. Before serving, let the muffins cool somewhat.

Spanish Chickpea and Spinach Pie

Ingredients:

- Chickpea flour
- Water
- Spinach
- Onion
- Garlic
- Olive oil
- Salt and pepper

Instructions:

1. Warm up the oven to 375°F (190°C) and coat a pie dish with oil.
2. To make a batter, combine chickpea flour and water in a bowl.
3. Add salt and pepper after sautéing the spinach, onion, and garlic in olive oil until they are wilted.
4. Transfer half of the batter into the pie dish that has been prepared, and then cover with the spinach mixture.
5. Cover the spinach mixture with the remaining batter, smoothing the top.
6. Bake for 30 to 35 minutes, or until the filling is set and the top is golden brown.

Spanish Rice Cake

Ingredients:

- Rice flour
- Sugar
- Eggs
- Milk
- Baking powder
- Vanilla extract
- Butter (for greasing)

Instructions:

1. Grease a cake pan with butter and preheat the oven to 350°F (175°C).
2. Combine rice flour, sugar, eggs, milk, baking powder, and vanilla extract in a mixing bowl and beat until smooth.
3. Transfer the mixture to the ready-made cake pan.
4. Bake the cake for thirty to thirty-five minutes or until a toothpick inserted in the centre comes out clean.
5. Allow the cake to cool completely before slicing and serving.

Spanish Buckwheat Pancakes

Ingredients:

- Buckwheat flour
- Milk
- Eggs
- Baking powder
- Salt
- Butter (for cooking)

Instructions:

1. Combine the buckwheat flour, baking powder, eggs, milk, and salt in a mixing dish and whisk until well combined.
2. In a skillet over medium heat, preheat the butter.
3. To make pancakes, pour batter onto the skillet.
4. Cook until surface bubbles appear, then turn and continue cooking until both sides are golden brown.
5. Proceed with the leftover batter, adjusting the amount of butter in the skillet as necessary.

Spanish Barley Bread

Ingredients:

- Barley flour
- Yeast
- Water
- Salt

Instructions:

1. Let the yeast dissolve in the warm water and leave it for five minutes.
2. Combine the yeast mixture, barley flour, and salt in a mixing dish.
3. Work the dough into an elastic and smooth texture.
4. Form the dough into a loaf, put it in a greased loaf pan, cover it, and allow it to rise until it doubles in size.
5. Bake for 40 to 45 minutes, or until the bread sounds hollow when tapped on the bottom, in an oven that has been set to 375°F (190°C).

Spanish Corn and Cheese Tart

Ingredients:

- Cornmeal
- Flour
- Butter
- Salt
- Water
- Corn kernels
- Cheese (such as Manchego or Cheddar)
- Eggs
- Milk

Instructions:

1. Grease a tart pan with butter and preheat the oven to 350°F (175°C).
2. Toss cornmeal, flour, butter, and salt in a bowl until crumbly. Gradually add water until a dough forms.
3. To create a crust, press the dough firmly into the tart pan's bottom and sides.
4. Evenly distribute grated cheese and corn kernels on the crust.
5. Whisk the eggs and milk in a separate bowl, then cover the corn and cheese with the mixture.
6. Bake for 30 to 35 minutes or until the crust is golden brown and the filling is set.

Spanish Spelt and Lemon Muffins

Ingredients:

- Spelt flour
- Sugar

- Eggs
- Milk
- Lemon zest
- Baking powder
- Olive oil

Instructions:

1. Adjust the oven temperature to 350°F (175°C) and place paper liners into a muffin tray.
2. Combine the spelt flour, sugar, eggs, milk, baking powder, lemon zest, and olive oil in a bowl and mix until well combined.
3. Fill each of the muffin tin cups to about two-thirds full with the batter.
4. Bake until a toothpick inserted into the centre comes out clean, about 15 to 20 minutes.
5. Before serving, let the muffins cool somewhat.

Spanish Quinoa and Vegetable Pie

Ingredients:

- Quinoa
- Mixed vegetables (such as bell peppers, zucchini, and carrots)
- Onion
- Garlic
- Olive oil
- Vegetable broth
- Eggs
- Cheese (optional)

Instructions:

1. Prepare the quinoa per the directions on the package and set it aside.
2. Saute garlic, onion, and mixed veggies in olive oil until they are soft.
3. Combine the cooked quinoa, eggs, cheese (if using), sauteed veggies, and vegetable broth in a bowl.
4. Transfer mixture to pie dish that has been oiled.
5. Bake until firm and tops are golden brown, 30 to 35 minutes.

CHAPTER - 10
GLUTEN-FREE AND VEGAN OPTIONS IN SPANISH BAKING

Vegan Torta de Santiago (Almond Cake)

Ingredients:

- Almond flour
- Sugar
- Olive oil
- Almond milk
- Lemon zest
- Baking powder
- Powdered sugar (for dusting)

Instructions:

1. Set the oven's temperature to 350°F, or 180°C. Oil and dust a cake pan.

2. Thoroughly mix almond flour, sugar, lemon zest, olive oil, almond milk, and baking powder in a bowl.
3. Transfer the mixture to the ready-made cake pan and level the surface.
4. Bake the cake for thirty to thirty-five minutes or until a toothpick inserted in the centre comes out clean.
5. After the cake has cooled thoroughly, dust it with powdered sugar and serve.

Gluten-free rosquillas (Doughnuts)

Ingredients:

- Gluten-free flour blend
- Baking powder
- Sugar
- Almond milk
- Lemon zest
- Sunflower oil (for frying)

Instructions:

1. Combine sugar, baking powder, and gluten-free flour in a bowl. Mix in the almond milk and lemon zest until a smooth dough forms.
2. Preheat 350°F (175°C) sunflower oil in a deep fryer or large pot.
3. Gently form the dough into tiny rings and place them into the boiling oil.
4. Fry till golden brown, take out, and place paper towels to drain.
5. Before serving, you may want to dust it with powdered sugar.

Vegan Magdalenas (Spanish Lemon Muffins)

Ingredients:

- All-purpose flour
- Baking powder
- Sugar
- Almond milk
- Lemon zest
- Olive oil

Instructions:

1. Turn the oven on to 375°F, or 190°C. Use paper liners to line a muffin tray.
2. Combine sugar, flour, and baking powder in a bowl. Stir together the lemon zest, olive oil, and almond milk.
3. Spoon the batter into each muffin cup, about 3/4 full.
4. Bake until a toothpick inserted into the centre comes out clean, about 15 to 20 minutes.
5. After the muffins have cooled in the pan for a few minutes, move them to a wire rack to finish cooling.

Gluten-Free Churros with Chocolate Sauce

Ingredients:

- Gluten-free all-purpose flour
- Baking powder
- Salt
- Water
- Olive oil
- Sugar
- Cinnamon

- Dark chocolate
- Coconut milk

Instructions:

1. Put the water, sugar, salt, and olive oil in a pot. Heat till boiling.
2. Lower the heat and stir continuously until a thick dough forms while gradually adding the gluten-free flour.
3. Spoon the dough into a piping bag and insert a star tip into it.
4. Preheat the oil in a big pot or deep fryer to 375°F (190°C).
5. Cut the dough strips with scissors as you pipe them straight into the heated oil and cook them till golden brown.
6. In a small dish, combine sugar and cinnamon. In the sugar mixture, roll the deep-fried churros.
7. To make the chocolate sauce, combine coconut milk and dark chocolate in a saucepan over low heat, stirring to combine. Warm up some chocolate sauce to dip the churros in.

Vegan Tarta de Manzana (Spanish Apple Tart)

Ingredients:

- Pie crust (vegan and gluten-free if desired)
- Apples
- Lemon juice
- Sugar
- Cinnamon
- Apricot jam (optional)

Instructions:

1. Turn the oven on to 375°F, or 190°C. Roll out your pie dough and place it inside a tart pan.
2. Core, peel, and thinly slice apples. Toss with sugar, cinnamon, and lemon juice.
3. Place the apple slices on the pie crust in concentric circles.
4. Bake for 30 to 35 minutes, or until the apples are soft and the crust is golden brown.
5. For a glossy finish, you can optionally reheat apricot jam and brush it over the tart's top.

Gluten-Free Torrijas (Spanish French Toast)

Ingredients:

- Gluten-free bread slices
- Almond milk
- Eggs (or vegan egg substitute)
- Sugar
- Cinnamon
- Olive oil (for frying)

Instructions:

1. Combine almond milk, sugar, cinnamon, and eggs (or vegan egg alternatives) in a small dish.
2. Coat both sides of the gluten-free bread slices with the mixture.
3. In a skillet over medium heat, preheat the olive oil. Slices of bread should be fried until golden brown on all sides.
4. Take out of the skillet and place on paper towels to drain.

5. If preferred, top warm food with more sugar and cinnamon.

Honey Pastries

Ingredients:

- All-purpose flour
- Baking powder
- Olive oil
- Orange juice
- Ground cinnamon
- Agave syrup (or maple syrup for a vegan option)

Instructions:

1. In a bowl, combine the flour, baking powder, orange juice, olive oil, and a dash of cinnamon. Work the dough until smooth.
2. Gently roll out the dough and cut it into tiny diamond or rectangular shapes.
3. In a skillet over medium heat, preheat the olive oil. Cook until all sides of the dough pieces are golden brown.
4. Take out of the skillet and place on paper towels to drain.
5. While still warm, drizzle with agave or maple syrup. Before serving, allow to cool.

Gluten-Free Piononos (Spanish Rolled Sponge Cake)

Ingredients:

- Gluten-free flour blend
- Baking powder
- Eggs

- Sugar
- Vanilla extract
- Whipped cream (vegan if desired)

Instructions:

1. Set the oven to 350°F or 180°C. Grease and place parchment paper on a baking sheet.
2. Beat eggs and sugar in a bowl until light and frothy. Blend in the vanilla extract.
3. Fold gently until just mixed after sifting in the baking powder and gluten-free flour.
4. Evenly spread out the batter on the baking sheet that has been prepared.
5. Bake the cake for ten to twelve minutes or until it is golden and pliable to the touch.
6. Take the cake out of the oven and allow it to cool somewhat. Cover the cake with whipped cream, then carefully roll it up.
7. Cut into rounds and present.

Vegan Bizcocho de Chocolate (Spanish Chocolate Cake)

Ingredients:

- All-purpose flour
- Cocoa powder
- Baking powder
- Sugar
- Olive oil
- Almond milk

Instructions:

1. Set the oven's temperature to 350°F, or 180°C. Oil and dust a cake pan.
2. Combine flour, sugar, baking powder, and cocoa powder in a bowl.
3. Until smooth, stir in almond milk and olive oil.
4. Transfer the mixture to the ready-made cake pan and level the surface.
5. Bake until a toothpick inserted into the centre comes out clean, 25 to 30 minutes.
6. After the cake has cooled in the pan for ten minutes, move it to a wire rack to finish cooling. Have fun!

Gluten-Free Empanadas de Fruta (Spanish Fruit Turnovers)

Ingredients:

- Gluten-free pie crust dough
- Assorted fruits (such as apples, pears, berries)
- Sugar
- Cinnamon
- Lemon juice

Instructions:

1. Turn the oven on to 375°F, or 190°C. Roll out the dough for the gluten-free pie crust and cut rounds out of it.
2. Combine the chopped fruits, sugar, cinnamon, and lemon juice in a bowl.
3. Spoon a heaping tablespoon of fruit filling into each dough circle. Using a fork, fold over and seal the edges.
4. Transfer the turnovers to a parchment paper-lined baking sheet.

5. Bake until golden brown, 20 to 25 minutes.
6. Let it cool a little bit before serving.

Vegan Polvorones (Spanish Shortbread Cookies)

Ingredients:

- All-purpose flour
- Almond flour
- Powdered sugar
- Olive oil
- Almond milk
- Ground cinnamon

Instructions:

1. Set the oven's temperature to 350°F, or 180°C. Use parchment paper to line a baking sheet.
2. Mix almond flour, powdered sugar, ground cinnamon, olive oil, almond milk, and all-purpose flour in a bowl. Stir to form a dough.
3. Using cookie cutters, roll out the dough and cut it into the desired shapes.
4. After arranging the cookies on the baking sheet, bake them for 12 to 15 minutes or until they are light golden.
5. After the cookies have cooled down on the baking sheet for a few minutes, move them to a wire rack to finish cooling.

Gluten-Free Bunuelos de Viento (Spanish Cream Puffs)

Ingredients:

- Gluten-free flour blend
- Baking powder
- Salt
- Water
- Olive oil
- Eggs
- Sugar
- Lemon zest

Instructions:

1. Put the water, sugar, salt, and olive oil in a pot. Heat till boiling.
2. Lower the heat and gradually whisk in the gluten-free flour until a smooth dough forms.
3. Turn off the heat and allow to cool somewhat. Next, beat each egg one at a time until well combined.
4. Drop dough spoonfuls into heated oil and cook until puffy and golden brown.
5. Before serving, drain on paper towels and dust with powdered sugar.

Vegan Mantecados (Spanish Crumbly Cookies)

Ingredients:

- All-purpose flour
- Almond flour
- Sugar
- Olive oil
- Almond milk
- Lemon zest
- Ground cinnamon

Instructions:

1. Set the oven's temperature to 350°F, or 180°C. Use parchment paper to line a baking sheet.
2. Mix the almond flour, sugar, ground cinnamon, lemon zest, olive oil, almond milk, and all-purpose flour in a bowl. Stir to form a dough.
3. Using the baking sheet that has been prepared, roll the dough into small balls and gently flatten them.
4. Bake until the sides are just beginning to turn brown, 12 to 15 minutes.
5. After the cookies have cooled down on the baking sheet for a few minutes, move them to a wire rack to finish cooling.

Gluten-Free Tarta de Santiago (Almond Tart)

Ingredients:

- Almond flour
- Sugar

- Eggs
- Lemon zest
- Almond extract
- Powdered sugar (for dusting)

Instructions:

1. Set the oven's temperature to 350°F, or 180°C. Dust and grease a tart pan.
2. Using a bowl, thoroughly mix the almond flour, sugar, eggs, lemon zest, and almond extract.
3. Transfer the batter to the tart pan that has been ready and level the top.
4. Bake the tart for 25 to 30 minutes or until it's firm and has a hint of colour.
5. Allow the dessert to cool fully before dusting it with powdered sugar and serving.

Vegan Leche Frita (Fried Milk Dessert)

Ingredients:

- Almond milk
- Cornstarch
- Sugar
- Cinnamon
- Lemon zest
- Cornmeal
- Olive oil (for frying)

Instructions:

1. Heat the almond milk, sugar, cinnamon, and lemon zest in a skillet until it almost boils.

2. Create a slurry by mixing cornstarch with a small amount of water in another basin.
3. Stirring continuously, gradually add the cornstarch slurry to the heated almond milk mixture until it thickens.
4. Transfer the mixture to a shallow plate and chill it until it solidifies.
5. Cut the solid mixture into squares, press them into heated olive oil until golden brown, then dust them with cornmeal.
6. Before serving, drain on paper towels and dust with cinnamon sugar.

CHAPTER - 11
BAKING WITH NUTS AND DRIED FRUITS

Almond and Orange Biscotti

Ingredients:

- 1 cup almonds, chopped
- 2 cups all-purpose flour
- 1 cup sugar
- 1 teaspoon baking powder
- 1/4 teaspoon salt
- 3 eggs
- 1 tablespoon orange zest
- 1 teaspoon vanilla extract

Instructions:

1. Preheat the oven to 350°F (175°C), and place parchment paper on a baking pan.

2. Put the flour, sugar, baking powder, and salt in a mixing basin.
3. Beat the eggs in another bowl and stir in the vanilla extract and orange zest.
4. Mixing gradually until a dough forms, add the dry ingredients to the liquid components.
5. Stir in almonds, chopped.
6. Split the dough in half, then form each half into a log on the baking sheet that has been ready.
7. Bake until firm and faintly golden, 25 to 30 minutes.
8. Take the dish out of the oven and let it cool for ten minutes. Then, lower the oven's setting to 325°F or 160°C.
9. Cut the logs into 1/2-inch-thick slices using a diagonal motion, then place them cut-side down on the baking pan.
10. Continue baking for ten to fifteen minutes or until the biscotti are golden and crisp. Before serving, allow it to cool fully.

Walnut and Fig Bread

Ingredients:

- 2 cups all-purpose flour
- 1 teaspoon baking powder
- 1/2 teaspoon baking soda
- 1/4 teaspoon salt
- 1/2 cup unsalted butter, softened
- 3/4 cup brown sugar
- 2 eggs
- 1 teaspoon vanilla extract
- 1 cup buttermilk
- 1 cup chopped walnuts

- 1 cup chopped dried figs

Instructions:

1. Grease a 9 by 5-inch loaf pan and preheat the oven to 350°F (175°C).
2. Combine the flour, baking soda, baking powder, and salt in a bowl.
3. Cream butter and brown sugar in a different, big dish until they are light and fluffy.
4. Add the vanilla essence after beating in the eggs one at a time.
5. Stir thoroughly to incorporate the dry components with the wet ingredients gradually, alternating with buttermilk.
6. Stir in the dried figs and chopped walnuts.
7. Transfer batter to loaf pan and level the top.
8. Bake for fifty to sixty minutes or until a toothpick inserted in the middle comes out clean.
9. After letting the bread set in the pan for ten minutes, move it to a wire rack to finish cooling before slicing.

Hazelnut Chocolate Chip Cookies

Ingredients:

- 1 cup hazelnuts, toasted and chopped
- 1 cup unsalted butter, softened
- 1 cup brown sugar
- 1/2 cup granulated sugar
- 2 eggs
- 1 teaspoon vanilla extract
- 2 cups all-purpose flour
- 1 teaspoon baking soda

- 1/2 teaspoon salt
- 1 1/2 cups semisweet chocolate chips

Instructions:

1. Preheat the oven to 350°F (175°C), and place parchment paper on the baking sheets.
2. Cream butter, brown sugar, and granulated sugar in a mixing dish until frothy and light.
3. Add the vanilla essence after beating in the eggs one at a time.
4. Combine the flour, baking soda, and salt in another basin.
5. Mix the dry ingredients until they are just incorporated, then gradually add them to the wet components.
6. Stir in chocolate chips and chopped hazelnuts.
7. Leaving space between each cookie, drop dough onto the baking sheets that have been prepared in rounded tablespoons.
8. Bake for ten to twelve minutes or until the edges are browned.
9. After a few minutes, let the cookies rest on the baking sheets before moving them to a wire rack to finish cooling.

Pine Nut Tart with Honey Glaze

Ingredients:

- 1 9-inch pie crust, homemade or store-bought
- 1 cup pine nuts
- 3/4 cup light corn syrup
- 1/4 cup honey
- 1/4 cup brown sugar
- 2 eggs

- 1 teaspoon vanilla extract
- Pinch of salt

Instructions:

1. Set oven temperature to 175°C/350°F.
2. Gently press the pie crust into a tart pan. Cut away any extra dough around the edges.
3. Combine brown sugar, honey, and corn syrup in a saucepan. Cook the sugar over medium heat until it dissolves.
4. Turn off the heat and allow to cool a little.
5. Combine eggs, salt, and vanilla essence in a bowl.
6. Beat the warm syrup mixture into the egg mixture gradually until thoroughly blended.
7. Add pine nuts and stir.
8. Fill the prepared pie shell with the contents.
9. Bake for thirty to thirty-five minutes or until the filling is golden brown and set.
10. Allow to cool fully before serving.

Pistachio Baklava Rolls

Ingredients:

- 1 package phyllo dough, thawed
- 1 1/2 cups shelled pistachios, chopped
- 1 cup unsalted butter, melted
- 1 cup sugar
- 1/2 cup water
- 1/4 cup honey
- 1 teaspoon lemon juice

Instructions:

1. Preheat the oven to 175°C/350°F, and lightly butter a baking dish.
2. Spread out a single phyllo dough sheet and drizzle it with melted butter.
3. Drizzle the buttered phyllo sheet with a layer of finely chopped pistachios.
4. Create a tight log out of the phyllo dough.
5. Repeat with the remaining pistachios and phyllo sheets.
6. Slice each roll into thin, two-inch-long pieces.
7. Slide the rolls into the baking dish that has been ready, seam side down.
8. Put the sugar, water, honey, and lemon juice in a pot. After bringing to a boil, lower heat and simmer for ten minutes.
9. Drizzle the baklava rolls with the syrup.
10. Bake for 25 to 30 minutes or until crispy and golden brown.
11. Before serving, let cool.

Cashew and Cranberry Scones

Ingredients:

- 2 cups all-purpose flour
- 1/4 cup granulated sugar
- 1 tablespoon baking powder
- 1/2 teaspoon salt
- 1/2 cup unsalted butter, cold and cubed
- 1/2 cup dried cranberries
- 1/2 cup chopped cashews
- 3/4 cup milk
- 1 teaspoon vanilla extract

- 1 egg, beaten (for egg wash)

Instructions:

1. Preheat the oven to 400°F (200°C) and place parchment paper on a baking pan.
2. Combine the flour, sugar, baking powder, and salt in a sizable bowl.
3. Using a pastry cutter or fork, cut in cold butter until the mixture resembles coarse crumbs.
4. Add chopped cashews and dried cranberries and stir.
5. Whisk milk and vanilla extract together in another basin.
6. Stirring just until mixed, gradually add the milk mixture to the dry ingredients.
7. Place the dough on a surface dusted with flour and gently work it into a cohesive ball.
8. Press the dough into an approximately 1-inch-thick circle.
9. Slicing the circle into eight wedges, place them on the ready baking sheet.
10. Use a beaten egg to brush the scones' tops lightly.
11. Bake until golden brown, 15 to 18 minutes.
12. Warm up and serve with jam or butter.

Macadamia Nut Brownies

Ingredients:

- 1 cup unsalted butter
- 2 cups granulated sugar
- 4 large eggs
- 1 teaspoon vanilla extract
- 1 cup all-purpose flour
- 3/4 cup unsweetened cocoa powder
- 1/2 teaspoon salt

- 1 cup chopped macadamia nuts

Instructions:

1. Preheat the oven to 350°F (175°C), and coat a 9-by-13-inch baking pan with butter.
2. Melt the butter in a saucepan over low heat.
3. Turn off the heat and thoroughly mix in the sugar.
4. Add the vanilla essence after beating in the eggs one at a time.
5. Sift the flour, salt, and cocoa powder in a separate bowl.
6. Mixing until just incorporated, gradually add the dry ingredients to the wet components.
7. Add chopped macadamia nuts and fold in.
8. Transfer the mixture to the baking pan that has been ready and level it out.
9. Bake for 25 to 30 minutes or until moist crumbs come out of a toothpick inserted into the centre.
10. Allow to fully cool before slicing into squares.

Pecan Maple Cinnamon Rolls

Ingredients:

For the dough:

- 1 cup warm milk
- 2 1/4 teaspoons active dry yeast
- 1/4 cup granulated sugar
- 1/2 cup unsalted butter, melted
- 2 large eggs
- 4 1/2 cups all-purpose flour
- 1 teaspoon salt

For the filling:

- 1/2 cup unsalted butter, softened
- 1/2 cup brown sugar
- 2 teaspoons ground cinnamon
- 1 cup chopped pecans

For the glaze:

- 1 cup powdered sugar
- 2 tablespoons maple syrup
- 2 tablespoons milk

Instructions:

1. Combine warm milk, granulated sugar, and yeast in a bowl. Stir until foamy, then let it sit for five to ten minutes.
2. Stir in eggs and melted butter.
3. Whisk the flour and salt together in another bowl.
4. Mixing gradually until a dough forms, add the dry ingredients to the liquid components.
5. Until the dough is smooth and elastic, knead it for about five minutes on a floured surface.
6. After the dough has doubled in size, please place it in a greased bowl, cover it with a fresh kitchen towel, and let it rise in a warm location for about an hour.
7. After the dough has risen, punch it down and roll it out into a big rectangle.
8. Cover the dough with softened butter and top with chopped pecans, cinnamon, and brown sugar.
9. Using the long side of the dough, tightly roll it up and cut it into 12 equal slices.
10. After the rolls have risen for 30 minutes, put them in a baking dish that has been buttered, cover it, and leave it.

11. Bake the rolls for 20 to 25 minutes, or until golden brown, after preheating the oven to 375°F (190°C).
12. Make the glaze by combining powdered sugar, maple syrup, and milk and whisking until smooth while the rolls bake.
13. Before serving, drizzle the glaze over the warm cinnamon rolls.

Chestnut Flour Cake with Raisins

Ingredients:

- 1 cup chestnut flour
- 1 cup all-purpose flour
- 1 teaspoon baking powder
- 1/2 teaspoon baking soda
- 1/4 teaspoon salt
- 1/2 cup unsalted butter, softened
- 1 cup granulated sugar
- 2 eggs
- 1 cup buttermilk
- 1 teaspoon vanilla extract
- 1 cup raisins

Instructions:

1. Grease a 9-inch round cake pan and preheat the oven to 350°F (175°C).
2. Combine the all-purpose flour, baking soda, baking powder, salt, and chestnut flour in a bowl.
3. Cream the butter and sugar in a different, big basin until they are light and creamy.
4. Add the vanilla essence after beating in the eggs one at a time.

5. Stir thoroughly to incorporate the dry components with the wet ingredients gradually, alternating with buttermilk.
6. Stir in the raisins.
7. Transfer the mixture to the ready-made cake pan and level the surface.
8. Bake for 35 to 40 minutes or until the middle comes out clean when a toothpick is inserted.
9. After 10 minutes of cooling in the pan, move the baked goods to a wire rack to finish cooling before slicing.

Apricot and Almond Croissants

Ingredients:

- 1 package (17.3 ounces) frozen puff pastry, thawed
- 1/2 cup apricot preserves
- 1/2 cup almond paste
- 1/4 cup sliced almonds
- 1 egg, beaten (for egg wash)
- Powdered sugar for dusting (optional)

Instructions:

1. Preheat the oven to 400°F (200°C) and place parchment paper on a baking pan.
2. Using a surface dusted with flour, roll out the thawed puff pastry into a sizable rectangle.
3. Make smaller triangles out of the rectangle.
4. Gently stir the almond paste and apricot preserves in a small basin until thoroughly mixed.
5. Put a dollop of the almond-pricot mixture onto the broad end of every triangle.

6. Starting from the wide end, tightly roll each triangle and lay them seam side down on the baking sheet that has been prepared.
7. Spread sliced almonds on top of the croissants after brushing them with beaten egg.
8. Bake for 15 to 20 minutes or until puffy and golden brown.
9. Allow to cool on the baking sheet for a few minutes, then move to a wire rack to finish cooling.
10. If preferred, sprinkle with powdered sugar prior to serving.

Date and Walnut Rugelach

Ingredients:

- 1 cup unsalted butter, softened
- 8 ounces cream cheese, softened
- 2 cups all-purpose flour
- 1/4 cup granulated sugar
- 1 teaspoon vanilla extract
- 1 cup chopped dates
- 1 cup chopped walnuts
- 1/4 cup brown sugar
- 1 teaspoon ground cinnamon

Instructions:

1. In a sizable bowl, blend cream cheese and butter until smooth.
2. Add the flour, sugar, and vanilla extract gradually while mixing to form a dough.
3. Split the dough into four equal pieces, cover each with plastic wrap, and chill for a minimum of 60 minutes.

4. Prepare the oven to 350°F (175°C) and place parchment paper on baking sheets.
5. Combine the chopped dates, chopped walnuts, cinnamon, and brown sugar in a small bowl.
6. Roll out a piece of dough into a circle on a surface that has been lightly dusted with flour.
7. Evenly distribute a quarter of the date-walnut mixture onto the circle of dough.
8. Create twelve equal wedges out of the circle.
9. Tightly roll each wedge, starting at the wide end and ending at the point.
10. Press the rugelach seam side down onto the baking sheets that have been prepared.
11. Proceed again using the leftover dough and filling.
12. Bake until golden brown, 20 to 25 minutes.
13. After a few minutes of cooling on the baking sheets, move them to a wire rack to finish cooling.

Brazil Nut and Coconut Macaroons

Ingredients:

- 3 cups shredded coconut
- 1 cup sweetened condensed milk
- 1 teaspoon vanilla extract
- 2/3 cup chopped Brazil nuts
- 2 egg whites
- Pinch of salt
- 1/4 cup granulated sugar

Instructions:

1. Prepare the oven to 325°F (160°C) and place parchment paper on baking sheets.

2. Using a bowl, thoroughly blend the sweetened condensed milk, vanilla essence, and shredded coconut.
3. Add chopped Brazil nuts and stir.
4. Beat the egg whites in another basin with a small teaspoon of salt until firm peaks form.
5. Until combined, gradually mix in the granulated sugar.
6. Until the coconut mixture is equally blended, gently fold in the beaten egg whites.
7. Spoon the mixture onto the baking sheets and space them apart with a spoon.
8. Bake the macaroons for 20 to 25 minutes or until the edges are golden brown.
9. After a few minutes, let the baked goods cool on the baking sheets before moving them to a wire rack to finish cooling.

Sesame Seed Brittle

Ingredients:

- 1 cup granulated sugar
- 1/2 cup water
- 1 cup sesame seeds
- 1 tablespoon unsalted butter
- 1/2 teaspoon vanilla extract
- 1/4 teaspoon baking soda

Instructions:

1. Place parchment paper on a baking pan and set it aside.
2. Place water and sugar in a heavy-bottomed saucepan and heat over medium heat.
3. Bring to a boil without stirring and stir until sugar is dissolved.

4. Simmer the mixture until it turns golden amber in colour or reaches 300°F (150°C) on a candy thermometer.
5. Quickly stir in butter, baking soda, vanilla essence, and sesame seeds.
6. Transfer the mixture to the baking sheet that has been ready and use a spatula to distribute it thinly.
7. Until it solidifies, let it cool fully at room temperature.
8. After the brittle has solidified, break it into pieces and store it in an airtight container.

Almond Butter Banana Bread

Ingredients:

- 2 cups all-purpose flour
- 1 teaspoon baking soda
- 1/2 teaspoon baking powder
- 1/2 teaspoon salt
- 1/2 cup unsalted butter, softened
- 3/4 cup granulated sugar
- 2 large eggs
- 3 ripe bananas, mashed
- 1/2 cup almond butter
- 1 teaspoon vanilla extract
- 1/2 cup chopped almonds (optional for topping)

Instructions:

1. Grease a 9 by 5-inch loaf pan and preheat the oven to 350°F (175°C).
2. Combine flour, baking powder, baking soda, and salt in a bowl.
3. Beat softened butter and sugar in a different, large basin until the mixture is light and fluffy.

4. Add the mashed bananas, almond butter, and vanilla extract after beating in the eggs one at a time.
5. Mix the dry ingredients until they are just incorporated, then gradually add them to the wet components.
6. Transfer the batter to the loaf pan that has been ready and level the top.
7. If using, sprinkle chopped almonds over the batter.
8. Bake for sixty to seventy minutes or until a toothpick inserted in the centre comes out tidy.
9. After 10 minutes of cooling in the pan, move the baked goods to a wire rack to finish cooling before slicing.

Peanut Butter and Jelly Thumbprint Cookies

Ingredients:

- 1 cup all-purpose flour
- 1/2 teaspoon baking powder
- 1/4 teaspoon salt
- 1/2 cup unsalted butter, softened
- 1/2 cup creamy peanut butter
- 1/2 cup granulated sugar
- 1/4 cup brown sugar
- 1 large egg
- 1 teaspoon vanilla extract
- 1/4 cup raspberry jam (or your favourite flavour)

Instructions:

1. Preheat oven to 350°F (175°C) and line baking sheets with parchment paper.
2. In a bowl, whisk together flour, baking powder, and salt.

3. In a separate large bowl, cream together softened butter, peanut butter, granulated sugar, and brown sugar until smooth.
4. Beat in egg and vanilla extract until well combined.
5. Gradually add the dry ingredients to the wet ingredients, mixing until a dough forms.
6. Roll tablespoonfuls of dough into balls and place them on the prepared baking sheets.
7. Use your thumb or the back of a spoon to make an indentation in the centre of each cookie.
8. Fill each indentation with a small spoonful of raspberry jam.
9. Bake for 10-12 minutes or until the cookies are set and lightly golden.
10. Let cool on the baking sheets for a few minutes before transferring to a wire rack to cool completely.

CHAPTER - 12
BREADSTICKS, CRACKERS, AND SNACK RECIPES

Traditional Spanish Breadsticks (Picos)

Ingredients:

- 2 cups all-purpose flour
- 1 teaspoon salt
- 1 teaspoon sugar
- 1 teaspoon active dry yeast
- 2/3 cup warm water
- Olive oil for brushing

- Coarse salt for sprinkling

Instructions:

1. Combine flour, sugar, yeast, and salt in a sizable mixing dish.
2. Add warm water gradually and stir until a dough forms.
3. Until the dough is smooth and elastic, knead it for five to seven minutes on a floured surface.
4. Separate the dough into tiny pieces and form each into a thin stick.
5. Arrange the breadsticks on a parchment paper-lined baking sheet.
6. Drizzle the breadsticks with a bit of olive oil and coarse salt.
7. Give the breadsticks thirty minutes or so to rise.
8. Set the oven's temperature to 200°C/400°F.
9. Bake the breadsticks for a golden brown colour for 12 to 15 minutes.
10. Take it out of the oven and let it cool down before serving.

Olive Oil and Rosemary Breadsticks

Ingredients:

- 2 cups all-purpose flour
- 1 teaspoon salt
- 1 teaspoon sugar
- 1 teaspoon active dry yeast
- 2/3 cup warm water
- 3 tablespoons olive oil
- 2 tablespoons chopped fresh rosemary
- Coarse salt for sprinkling

Instructions:

1. Follow steps 1-4 from the Traditional Spanish Breadsticks recipe.
2. In a small bowl, mix olive oil and chopped rosemary.
3. Brush the rolled breadsticks with the olive oil mixture.
4. Sprinkle with coarse salt.
5. Follow steps 7-10 from the Traditional Spanish Breadsticks recipe.

Garlic Parmesan Breadsticks

Ingredients:

- 2 cups all-purpose flour
- 1 teaspoon salt
- 1 teaspoon sugar
- 1 teaspoon active dry yeast
- 2/3 cup warm water
- 3 tablespoons butter, melted
- 2 cloves garlic, minced
- 1/4 cup grated Parmesan cheese
- 1 tablespoon chopped parsley
- Coarse salt for sprinkling

Instructions:

1. Proceed with the Traditional Spanish Breadsticks recipe, following steps 1-4.
2. Combine melted butter, finely chopped parsley, grated Parmesan cheese, and minced garlic in a small bowl.
3. Use the garlic-Parmesan butter mixture to brush the rolled breadsticks.
4. Add a little coarse salt.

5. Proceed with steps 7 through 10 of the recipe for Traditional Spanish Breadsticks.

Tomato Basil Breadsticks

Ingredients:

- 2 cups all-purpose flour
- 1 teaspoon salt
- 1 teaspoon sugar
- 1 teaspoon active dry yeast
- 2/3 cup warm water
- 3 tablespoons tomato paste
- 2 tablespoons chopped fresh basil
- 2 tablespoons grated Parmesan cheese
- Coarse salt for sprinkling

Instructions:

1. Proceed with the Traditional Spanish Breadsticks recipe, following steps 1-4.
2. Combine grated Parmesan cheese, chopped basil, and tomato paste in a small basin.
3. Cover the wrapped breadsticks with the tomato-basil mixture.
4. Add a little coarse salt.
5. Proceed with steps 7 through 10 of the recipe for Traditional Spanish Breadsticks.

Saffron and Sesame Seed Breadsticks

Ingredients:

- 2 cups all-purpose flour
- 1 teaspoon salt

- 1 teaspoon sugar
- 1 teaspoon active dry yeast
- 2/3 cup warm water
- 1/4 teaspoon saffron threads, crushed and dissolved in 1 tablespoon warm water
- 2 tablespoons sesame seeds
- Coarse salt for sprinkling

Instructions:

1. Add the dissolved saffron to the warm water and proceed as directed in steps 1-4 of the recipe for Traditional Spanish Breadsticks.
2. Drizzle the wrapped breadsticks with sesame seeds.
3. Proceed with steps 7 through 10 of the recipe for Traditional Spanish Breadsticks.

Chorizo and Manchego Cheese Breadsticks

Ingredients:

- 2 cups all-purpose flour
- 1 teaspoon salt
- 1 teaspoon sugar
- 1 teaspoon active dry yeast
- 2/3 cup warm water
- 1/4 cup finely chopped chorizo
- 1/4 cup grated Manchego cheese
- Coarse salt for sprinkling

Instructions:

1. Proceed with the Traditional Spanish Breadsticks recipe, following steps 1-4.

2. Top the rolled breadsticks with grated Manchego cheese and finely diced chorizo.
3. Proceed with steps 7 through 10 of the recipe for Traditional Spanish Breadsticks.

Spanish Tapenade Breadsticks

Ingredients:

- 2 cups all-purpose flour
- 1 teaspoon salt
- 1 teaspoon sugar
- 1 teaspoon active dry yeast
- 2/3 cup warm water
- 1/2 cup Spanish olive tapenade
- Coarse salt for sprinkling

Instructions:

1. Proceed with the Traditional Spanish Breadsticks recipe, following steps 1-4.
2. Drizzle the wrapped breadsticks with Spanish olive tapenade.
3. Proceed with steps 7 through 10 of the recipe for Traditional Spanish Breadsticks.

Paprika and Sea Salt Breadsticks

Ingredients:

- 2 cups all-purpose flour
- 1 teaspoon salt
- 1 teaspoon sugar
- 1 teaspoon active dry yeast
- 2/3 cup warm water

- 2 teaspoons smoked paprika
- Coarse sea salt for sprinkling

Instructions:

1. Proceed with the Traditional Spanish Breadsticks recipe, following steps 1-4.
2. Dust the rolled breadsticks with smoked paprika.
3. Proceed with steps 7 through 10 of the recipe for Traditional Spanish Breadsticks.

Fennel and Black Pepper Breadsticks

Ingredients:

- 2 cups all-purpose flour
- 1 teaspoon salt
- 1 teaspoon sugar
- 1 teaspoon active dry yeast
- 2/3 cup warm water
- 1 tablespoon fennel seeds
- 1 teaspoon coarsely ground black pepper
- Coarse salt for sprinkling

Instructions:

1. Proceed with the Traditional Spanish Breadsticks recipe, following steps 1-4.
2. Dust the wrapped breadsticks with roughly ground black pepper and fennel seeds.
3. Proceed with steps 7 through 10 of the recipe for Traditional Spanish Breadsticks.

Spanish Cheese Crackers

Ingredients:

- 1 1/2 cups all-purpose flour
- 1/2 teaspoon salt
- 1/2 teaspoon smoked paprika
- 1/4 teaspoon garlic powder
- 1/2 cup grated Manchego cheese
- 1/4 cup cold unsalted butter, cut into small pieces
- 3-4 tablespoons cold water

Instructions:

1. Pulse the flour, salt, garlic powder, and smoked paprika in a food processor.
2. Include the grated Manchego cheese and pulse to mix it in.
3. Add the cold butter pieces and process the mixture until it looks like coarse crumbs.
4. Pulse the dough until it comes together gradually, adding 1 tablespoon at a time of cold water.
5. Press the dough into a disk, cover it with plastic wrap, and chill it for half an hour.
6. Adjust an oven thermometer to 375°F (190°C) and place parchment paper on a baking sheet.
7. Roll out the dough to a thickness of about 1/8 inch on a surface dusted with flour.
8. Shape the dough into the shapes you like with a knife or cookie cutter.
9. Arrange the crackers on the baking sheet that has been prepared, giving each one a fork prick.
10. Bake for 12 to 15 minutes or until crisp and golden brown.

11. Before serving, let the crackers cool fully.

Spicy Chorizo Crackers

Ingredients:

- 1 1/2 cups all-purpose flour
- 1/2 teaspoon salt
- 1/2 teaspoon smoked paprika
- 1/4 teaspoon cayenne pepper
- 1/4 cup finely chopped chorizo
- 1/4 cup cold unsalted butter, cut into small pieces
- 3-4 tablespoons cold water

Instructions:

1. Comply with the Spanish Cheese Crackers recipe, stages 1 through 5.
2. Toss in the finely chopped chorizo and pulse to mix it in.
3. Adhere to the Spanish Cheese Crackers recipe's stages 6 through 11.

Tomato and Oregano Crackers

Ingredients:

- 1 1/2 cups all-purpose flour
- 1/2 teaspoon salt
- 1/2 teaspoon dried oregano
- 2 tablespoons tomato paste
- 1/4 cup cold unsalted butter, cut into small pieces
- 3-4 tablespoons cold water

Instructions:

1. Proceed with the Spanish Cheese Crackers recipe, following steps 1-4.
2. Pulse the dough after adding the tomato paste and dry oregano.
3. Adhere to the Spanish Cheese Crackers recipe's stages 6 through 11.

Manchego and Chive Crackers

Ingredients:

- 1 1/2 cups all-purpose flour
- 1/2 teaspoon salt
- 1/2 teaspoon garlic powder
- 1/2 cup grated Manchego cheese
- 2 tablespoons finely chopped chives
- 1/4 cup cold unsalted butter, cut into small pieces
- 3-4 tablespoons cold water

Instructions:

1. Pulse the flour, salt, and garlic powder in a food processor.
2. Pulse in finely chopped chives and grated Manchego cheese until blended.
3. Add the cold butter pieces and process the mixture until it looks like coarse crumbs.
4. Pulse the dough until it comes together gradually, adding 1 tablespoon at a time of cold water.
5. Press the dough into a disk, cover it with plastic wrap, and chill it for half an hour.
6. Adjust an oven thermometer to 375°F (190°C) and place parchment paper on a baking sheet.

7. Roll out the dough to a thickness of about 1/8 inch on a surface dusted with flour.
8. Shape the dough into the shapes you like with a knife or cookie cutter.
9. Arrange the crackers on the baking sheet that has been prepared, giving each one a fork prick.
10. Bake for 12 to 15 minutes or until crisp and golden brown.
11. Before serving, let the crackers cool fully.

Spanish Almond Crackers

Ingredients:

- 1 cup almond flour
- 1/2 teaspoon salt
- 1/2 teaspoon smoked paprika
- 1/4 teaspoon garlic powder
- 1 large egg
- 1 tablespoon olive oil
- 1 tablespoon water
- Coarse salt for sprinkling

Instructions:

1. Place the almond flour, salt, garlic powder, and smoked paprika in a mixing bowl.
2. Mix the dry ingredients with the egg, water, and olive oil until a dough forms.
3. Roll the dough into a ball, cover with plastic wrap, and chill for half an hour.
4. Adjust the oven temperature to 350°F (175°C) and place parchment paper on a baking pan.

5. Roll out the dough to a thickness of about 1/8 inch on a surface dusted with flour.
6. Shape the dough into the shapes you like using a knife or cookie cutter.
7. Spread the crackers out on the baking sheet that has been prepared and sprinkle with coarse salt.
8. Bake for crisp and golden brown, 10 to 12 minutes.
9. Before serving, let the crackers cool fully.

Spanish Style Popcorn Snack

Ingredients:

- 1/2 cup popcorn kernels
- 2 tablespoons olive oil
- 1 teaspoon smoked paprika
- 1/2 teaspoon garlic powder
- 1/2 teaspoon salt

Instructions:

1. In a big pot over medium heat, warm the olive oil.
2. Include the popcorn kernels and place a lid on them.
3. Cook, periodically shaking the pot, until the popping stops.
4. Take the popcorn off of the burner and place it in a big bowl.
5. Combine the salt, garlic powder, and smoked paprika in a small bowl.
6. Drizzle the popcorn with olive oil and then top with the spice blend.
7. Toss the popcorn to coat it evenly.
8. Before serving, let the popcorn cool somewhat.

CHAPTER - 13

HERITAGE RECIPES

Spanish Potato Omelette

Ingredients:

- 4 large potatoes, peeled and thinly sliced
- 1 large onion, thinly sliced
- 6 eggs
- Salt, to taste
- Olive oil

Instructions:

1. In a big skillet over medium heat, warm the olive oil.
2. Add the onions and potato slices to the skillet and heat, turning periodically, until the potatoes are soft and starting to brown.
3. Beat the eggs and salt together in another basin.
4. Take the potatoes and onions out of the skillet and pour off any extra oil when they are done.
5. Mix thoroughly after adding the potatoes and onions to the beaten eggs.
6. In the skillet, preheat a small amount of additional olive oil over medium heat.
7. Transfer the potato and egg mixture to the skillet, making sure to distribute it uniformly.
8. Cook the omelette until the bottom is set, which should take a few minutes.
9. Using a plate or lid, carefully flip the omelette over and continue cooking until the second side is set and just beginning to brown.

10. Cut the tortilla española into wedges and serve hot or room temperature.

Churros with Chocolate Sauce

Ingredients:

- 1 cup water
- 2 tablespoons white sugar
- 1/2 teaspoon salt
- 2 tablespoons vegetable oil
- 1 cup all-purpose flour
- Oil for frying
- 1/2 cup white sugar
- 1 teaspoon ground cinnamon

For Chocolate Sauce:

- 1 cup semisweet chocolate chips
- 1/2 cup heavy cream

Instructions:

1. Combine water, salt, two teaspoons of sugar, and two tablespoons of vegetable oil in a small pot. Bring to a boil, then turn off the heat.
2. Until the mixture forms a ball, stir in flour.
3. Preheat the oil in a deep skillet or deep fryer to 375 degrees Fahrenheit (190 degrees Celsius). I use a pastry bag to pipe dough strips into the heated oil. When golden, fry them and then drain on paper towels.
4. Mix cinnamon and 1/2 cup sugar. Dredge the drained churros in a combination of sugar and cinnamon.
5. To make the chocolate sauce, bring the heavy cream to a simmer in a small saucepan.

6. Cover the chocolate chips with the heated cream and allow to stand for one minute.
7. Until the sauce is smooth and the chocolate chips have melted completely, stir the mixture.
8. Present the warm churros with dipping chocolate sauce.

Galician Turnovers

Ingredients:

- 2 cups all-purpose flour
- 1/2 teaspoon salt
- 1/2 cup unsalted butter, cold and cubed
- 1/2 cup cold water
- 1 tablespoon olive oil
- 1 onion, chopped
- 2 cloves garlic, minced
- 1 bell pepper, diced
- 1 tomato, diced
- 1/2 teaspoon paprika
- Salt and pepper, to taste
- 1 cup cooked shredded chicken or beef
- 1/4 cup pitted green olives, sliced
- 2 hard-boiled eggs, chopped
- Egg wash (1 egg beaten with 1 tablespoon water)

Instructions:

1. Place the flour and salt in a big bowl and stir until the mixture resembles coarse crumbs, cut in the butter.
2. Add the cold water gradually while mixing the dough until it comes together. Roll the dough into a ball, wrap it in plastic wrap, and refrigerate it for at least half an hour.
3. Heat the olive oil in a skillet over medium heat. Add the bell pepper, onion, and garlic and cook until tender.

4. Include the tomato, paprika, salt, and pepper. Cook the mixture until it thickens.
5. Turn off the heat and toss in the chopped, hard-boiled eggs, olives, and shredded beef or chicken. Allow the filling to cool.
6. Set oven temperature to 190°C/375°F. Use parchment paper to line a baking sheet.
7. Using a surface dusted with flour, roll out the cold dough to about 1/4 inch thick. Cut out circles using a glass or a round cutter.
8. Centre each dough circle with a teaspoon of the filling. Using a fork, fold the half-moon-shaped dough over the filling to seal the edges.
9. Put the empanadas onto the ready baking sheet. Use egg wash on the tops.
10. Bake until golden brown, 20 to 25 minutes. Warm up and serve.

Almond Cake from Santiago

Ingredients:

- 1 cup almond flour
- 1 cup sugar
- 4 eggs
- Zest of 1 lemon
- Zest of 1 orange
- 1/2 teaspoon ground cinnamon
- Powdered sugar for dusting

Instructions:

1. Set the oven temperature to 175°C or 350°F. Butter and dust a 9-inch circular cake pan.

2. In a sizable basin, thoroughly mix almond flour, sugar, eggs, orange and lemon zest, and cinnamon.
3. Transfer the mixture to the ready-made cake pan and level the surface.
4. Bake until a toothpick inserted into the centre comes out clean, about 25 to 30 minutes.
5. After the cake has cooled in the pan for ten minutes, move it to a wire rack to finish cooling.
6. After the cake has cooled, sprinkle powdered sugar on top. Allow to settle at room temperature.

Aniseed Donuts

Ingredients:

- 2 cups all-purpose flour
- 1/2 cup sugar
- 2 teaspoons baking powder
- 1/2 teaspoon salt
- 2 tablespoons anise seeds
- 2 eggs
- 1/4 cup milk
- 1/4 cup vegetable oil
- Oil for frying
- Additional sugar for coating

Instructions:

1. Combine the flour, sugar, baking powder, salt, and anise seeds in a sizable basin.
2. Beat the eggs in a different bowl and mix in the milk and vegetable oil.
3. Stir the dry ingredients into the wet mixture gradually until a dough forms.

4. Place the dough on a lightly floured surface and knead it gently until smooth.
5. Form the dough into tiny balls and then slightly flatten them to resemble doughnuts.
6. Preheat the oil in a deep skillet or fryer to 350°F (175°C).
7. Fry the doughnuts in batches, turning them once, until they turn golden brown.
8. While still warm, drain the cooked doughnuts on paper towels and then coat them in sugar.
9. Serve the room temperature or warm anise doughnuts.

Honey-Drizzled Fritters

Ingredients:

- 2 cups all-purpose flour
- 1 teaspoon baking powder
- 1/2 teaspoon salt
- 1/4 cup unsalted butter, melted
- 1/2 cup white wine
- Vegetable oil for frying
- Honey, for drizzling

Instructions:

1. Combine the flour, baking powder, and salt in a sizable bowl.
2. Until a dough forms, stir in melted butter and white wine.
3. Place the dough onto a surface dusted with flour and knead it until it becomes smooth.
4. Cut the dough into tiny pieces, then roll each one into a slender circle.
5. Preheat the oil to 375°F (190°C) in a deep fryer or deep skillet.

6. Fry the dough rounds in batches, turning them once until they are puffy and golden brown.
7. While still warm, drain the cooked fritters on paper towels and then drizzle with honey.
8. Serve the warm pestiños.

Spiral-Shaped Sweet Pastry

Ingredients:

- 4 cups bread flour
- 1/2 cup sugar
- 1 tablespoon instant yeast
- 1/2 teaspoon salt
- 1 cup warm milk
- 1/2 cup unsalted butter, melted
- 2 eggs
- Powdered sugar for dusting

Instructions:

1. Combine flour, sugar, instant yeast, and salt in a large bowl.
2. Create a well in the middle and add the eggs, melted butter, and warm milk. Stir to form a dough.
3. Place the dough on a lightly floured board and work it into an elastic and smooth texture.
4. Split the dough into four equal pieces, then roll each into a ball. Cover and let it rest for ten minutes.
5. Each ball of dough should be rolled into a thin rectangle and rolled into a tight spiral.
6. Transfer spirals to oiled baking sheets, cover, and allow them to rise until doubled in size, about 1 hour.
7. Set the oven to 175°C/350°F.

8. Bake the ensaimadas until golden brown, 20 to 25 minutes.
9. Before serving, allow the pastries to cool somewhat and then sprinkle with powdered sugar. Have fun!

Midsummer Cake

Ingredients:

- 500g bread flour
- 250ml warm water
- 25g fresh yeast
- 100g sugar
- 100ml olive oil
- Zest of 1 lemon
- Zest of 1 orange
- A pinch of salt
- 100g candied fruit (optional)
- 100g pine nuts (optional)

Instructions:

1. Add a small amount of sugar to warm water and dissolve the yeast. Give it a 10-minute rest period to get foamy.
2. Place the flour, sugar, olive oil, orange and lemon zest, and salt in a sizable mixing basin.
3. Until you have a smooth dough, gradually incorporate the yeast mixture into the flour mixture and knead. If using, stir in the pine nuts and candied fruit.
4. After the dough has doubled in size, cover it with a fresh kitchen towel and let it rise in a warm location for one to one and a half hours.
5. Set the oven's temperature to 180°C (350°F).
6. Press the risen dough into a circular cake. Transfer it to a parchment-lined baking sheet.

7. Bake the cake for 25 to 30 minutes or until it is hollow to the touch and golden brown.
8. Becolourcutting and serving, allow it to cool.

Spanish Crumbly Shortbread

Ingredients:

- 250g all-purpose flour
- 125g lard or vegetable shortening
- 125g sugar
- 1/2 teaspoon ground cinnamon (optional)
- Zest of 1 lemon (optional)
- Powdered sugar for dusting

Instructions:

1. Preheat the oven to 180°C (350°F) and place parchment paper on a baking pan.
2. Cream the sugar and lard (or vegetable shortening) in a mixing bowl until light and fluffy.
3. Until a dough forms, gradually add the flour, cinnamon (if used), and lemon zest (if using) to the creamed mixture and stir.
4. Shape the dough into little cakes or roll it into balls, then transfer them to the ready baking sheet.
5. Bake the mantecados for 15 to 20 minutes or until they are starting to become golden.
6. After a few minutes, let them cool on the baking sheet before moving them to a wire rack to finish cooling.
7. Before serving, sprinkle the mantecados with powdered sugar after they have cooled.

Spanish Cinnamon Cookies

Ingredients:

- 250g all-purpose flour
- 125g lard or vegetable shortening
- 75g powdered sugar
- 1/2 teaspoon ground cinnamon
- 50g almonds, finely chopped
- Powdered sugar for dusting

Instructions:

1. Preheat the oven to 180°C (350°F) and place parchment paper on a baking pan.
2. Using a mixing dish, thoroughly mix the powdered sugar and lard (or veggie shortening).
3. Until a crumbly dough develops, gradually add the flour, chopped almonds, and ground cinnamon to the creamed mixture and stir.
4. Using a floured surface, roll out the dough to a thickness of about 1/2 inch.
5. Cut the dough into squares or rectangles by using cookie cutters to cut out shapes.
6. After arranging the cookies on the baking sheet, bake them for 12 to 15 minutes or until they begin to become a light golden colour.
7. After a few minutes of cooling on the baking sheet, move the polvorones to a wire rack to finish cooling.
8. Before serving, sprinkle the polvorones with powdered sugar once they have cooled.

Sponge Cake Rolls from Santa Fe

Ingredients: For the sponge cake:

- 6 eggs
- 150g sugar
- 150g all-purpose flour
- 1 teaspoon vanilla extract
- For the filling:
- 250ml heavy cream
- 50g powdered sugar
- 1 teaspoon vanilla extract
- 50g chopped nuts (optional)

Instructions:

1. Turn the oven on to 180°C (350°F) and lightly oil a 9 by 13-inch baking sheet. Put parchment paper inside.
2. Beat the eggs and sugar in a sizable mixing bowl until light and frothy.
3. Until just mixed, gently fold in the flour and vanilla extract.
4. Transfer the batter to the baking sheet that has been ready and level it out.
5. Bake for 10 to 12 minutes, or until the sponge cake bounces back when you touch it and is lightly yellow.
6. Carefully wrap up the cake and the parchment paper from the short end while it's still warm. Allow it to cool fully.
7. Beat the heavy cream, powdered sugar, and vanilla extract in a separate dish until stiff peaks form.
8. Gently unfold the sponge cake that has cooled down and equally distributes the whipped cream filling on top. If using, scatter some chopped nuts on top.

9. Before slicing and serving, roll the cake firmly again and place it in the refrigerator for at least an hour.

Catalan Cream

Ingredients:

- 1-liter milk
- Zest of 1 lemon
- Zest of 1 orange
- 1 cinnamon stick
- 6 egg yolks
- 150g sugar
- 40g cornstarch
- Caster sugar for caramelizing

Instructions:

1. Place the milk, orange zest, and cinnamon stick in a saucepan and cook over medium heat until it almost boils. Take it off the stove and steep it for fifteen minutes or so.
2. Combine the egg yolks, sugar, and cornstarch in a mixing basin and whisk until thoroughly mixed.
3. While continuously whisking, gradually add the heated milk to the egg yolk mixture.
4. Transfer the mixture back to the pot and cook, stirring continually, over low heat until it thickens and coats the spoon's back.
5. Turn off the heat and sieve the custard to get rid of the cinnamon stick and zest.
6. Transfer the custard to separate serving bowls and let it come to room temperature. Next, chill for a minimum of two hours or until solidified.
7. Dust each custard with a small amount of caster sugar just before serving.

8. Using a kitchen torch or the broiler, caramelize the sugar until it melts and forms a golden crust on the dishes.
9. Before serving, let the crema Catalana sit for a minute so the caramel can solidify.

Butter Cake from Cantabria

Ingredients:

- 250g unsalted butter, softened
- 200g sugar
- 4 eggs
- 250g all-purpose flour
- 1 teaspoon baking powder
- Zest of 1 lemon
- Powdered sugar for dusting

Instructions:

1. Adjust the oven temperature to 180°C (350°F) and lightly oil a loaf pan.
2. Cream the butter and sugar in a mixing bowl until the mixture is light and fluffy.
3. Add the eggs one at a time, beating thoroughly after each one.
4. Add the flour and baking powder to the butter mixture gradually and stir until thoroughly mixed. Sift the ingredients together.
5. Add the lemon zest and stir.
6. Transfer the batter to the loaf pan that has been ready and use a spatula to level the top.
7. Bake for forty-five to forty-five minutes or until a toothpick inserted in the middle comes out clean.
8. After allowing the soba pasiego to cool in the pan for ten minutes, move it to a wire rack to finish cooling.

9. Before serving, dust with powdered sugar.

King's Cake

Ingredients:

For the dough:

- 500g bread flour
- 100g sugar
- 100g unsalted butter, softened
- 3 eggs
- Zest of 1 orange
- Zest of 1 lemon
- 1 teaspoon vanilla extract
- 10g active dry yeast
- 100ml warm milk

For the decoration:

- Candied fruit (e.g., orange peel, cherries)
- Sliced almonds
- Powdered sugar
- 1 egg, beaten

Instructions:

1. Dissolve the yeast in a small basin of warm milk with a small amount of sugar. Allow it to sit until foamy, about ten minutes.
2. Place the flour, sugar, eggs, softened butter, orange and lemon zests, vanilla extract, and yeast mixture in a large mixing bowl.
3. Work the dough into an elastic and smooth texture. Place a fresh kitchen towel over the bowl and let it rise in a

warm location until it has doubled in size, around one to two hours.

4. Form the risen dough into a ring by punching it down and creating a hole in the middle. Transfer it to a parchment paper-lined baking sheet.
5. Set the oven's temperature to 180°C (350°F).
6. Use a beaten egg to brush the top of the dough and garnish it with sliced almonds and candied fruit.
7. Bake for 25 to 30 minutes or until the roscón is hollow to the touch and has a golden brown colour.
8. Allow it to cool fully before applying a powdered sugar dusting.

Almond Confectionery

Ingredients:

- 250g almonds, blanched and peeled
- 200g sugar
- 1 egg
- 1/2 teaspoon lemon zest
- Pinch of salt
- Pine nuts for decoration

Instructions:

1. Preheat the oven to 180°C (350°F) and place parchment paper on a baking pan.
2. Using a food processor, finely grind the blanched almonds.
3. Put the ground almonds, sugar, egg, lemon zest, and salt in a mixing dish. Mix until a smooth dough forms.
4. Roll the dough into little balls and arrange them on the ready baking sheet.

5. To decorate each panellet, press a few pine nuts into the top.
6. Bake the panellets for a light golden color for 12 to 15 minutes.
7. After a few minutes, let them cool on the baking sheet before moving them to a wire rack to finish cooling.

Almond and Pumpkin Seed Pastries

Ingredients:

- 250g ground almonds
- 100g pumpkin seeds, toasted and ground
- 150g sugar
- 2 eggs
- Zest of 1 lemon
- Zest of 1 orange
- 1/2 teaspoon ground cinnamon
- 1/4 teaspoon ground cloves
- 1/4 teaspoon ground nutmeg
- Pinch of salt

Instructions:

1. Preheat the oven to 180°C (350°F) and place parchment paper on a baking pan.
2. Place the ground almonds, ground pumpkin seeds, sugar, orange and lemon zest, ground cloves, ground nutmeg, ground cinnamon, and ground salt in a mixing dish.
3. Gently beat the eggs and whisk them into the dry ingredients. Stir until a thick dough forms.
4. Using a floured surface, roll out the dough to a thickness of about 1/4 inch.

5. You may also cut the dough into squares or rectangles using a cookie cutter.
6. After transferring the pastries to the prepared baking sheet, bake them for 12 to 15 minutes or until they begin to become a light golden colour.
7. After a few minutes, let the fardelejos cool on the baking sheet before moving them to a wire rack to finish cooling.

CHAPTER - 14
SAVORY BAKES FROM SPAIN

Tortilla Espanola (Omelette)

Ingredients:

- 4 medium potatoes, peeled and thinly sliced
- 1 onion, thinly sliced
- 6 large eggs
- Salt to taste
- Olive oil for frying

Instructions:

1. Heat the olive oil in a large pan over medium heat. When the potatoes are cooked, add the onions and potatoes, season with salt, and simmer for ten to twelve minutes.
2. In another bowl, add salt and beat the eggs.
3. Gently mix the cooked potatoes and onions into the beaten eggs.
4. Pour the egg mixture into the skillet along with a little amount of more hot olive oil.

5. After the tortilla has cooked through and the bottom has firmed, carefully rotate it using a plate or cover. Cook until the other side of the tortilla sets, and the tortilla is cooked through.
6. After removing the heat source, let the food cool down a little bit before slicing and serving.

Galician Empanadas

Ingredients:

For the dough:

- 3 cups all-purpose flour
- 1 teaspoon salt
- ½ cup cold water
- ½ cup olive oil

For the filling:

- 2 cans of tuna, drained
- 1 onion, chopped
- 2 red bell peppers, chopped
- 2 tomatoes, chopped
- Salt and pepper to taste
- Olive oil for frying

Instructions:

1. In a bowl, combine flour and salt to make dough. Gradually add the olive oil and water while kneading the dough until it becomes smooth. After 30 minutes, cover it and let it rest.
2. In the interim, prepare the filling. In a skillet with heated olive oil, sauté onions and peppers until tender. Add the

tuna, tomatoes, pepper, and salt. Simmer for an additional five minutes. Could you turn off the heat and let it cool?

3. Set oven temperature to 190°C/375°F.
4. Separate the dough into two halves. Roll out each piece to form a slender circle.
5. Transfer one dough circle to a baking sheet. Leaving a thin border all the way around the edges, evenly distribute the filling over the dough.
6. Place the second circle of dough on top and press the sides together to seal.
7. Bake until golden brown, 30 to 35 minutes. Before slicing and serving, let it cool.

Catalan Flatbread with Roasted Vegetables

Ingredients:

For the dough:

- 3 cups all-purpose flour
- 1 teaspoon salt
- 1 tablespoon active dry yeast
- 1 cup warm water
- 2 tablespoons olive oil

For the topping:

- 2 red bell peppers, roasted and sliced
- 1 onion, thinly sliced
- 2 tomatoes, thinly sliced
- Salt and pepper to taste
- Olive oil for drizzling
- Optional: anchovy fillets, olives, or cooked sausage slices

Instructions:

1. Dissolve the yeast in the warm water in a basin. Wait five minutes for it to get frothy.
2. Combine flour and salt in another bowl. Add the olive oil and the yeast mixture. Work the dough until it becomes smooth. For one hour, cover it and let it rise in a warm location.
3. Set oven temperature to 200°C/400°F.
4. Flatten the dough and place it on a baking sheet in the shape of a big circle or rectangle.
5. Top the dough with the roasted peppers, onions, and tomatoes. Add pepper and salt for seasoning.
6. If desired, add any additional toppings.
7. Brush the crust with olive oil and bake for twenty to twenty-five minutes or until golden brown.
8. Before slicing and serving, allow it to cool slightly.

Cornbread

Ingredients:

-   1 cup cornmeal
-   1 cup all-purpose flour
-   1 tablespoon baking powder
-   1 teaspoon salt
-   ½ cup sugar
-   1 cup milk
-   2 eggs
-   ½ cup vegetable oil

Instructions:

1. Set oven temperature to 190°C/375°F. Butter a 9 x 9-inch baking pan.

2. Combine cornmeal, flour, baking powder, sugar, and salt in a bowl.
3. Combine the eggs, milk, and vegetable oil in a separate bowl.
4. Stir the dry ingredients thoroughly before progressively adding the wet ingredients.
5. Fill the baking dish with the batter.
6. Bake until a toothpick inserted into the centre comes out clean, 25 to 30 minutes.
7. Before cutting and serving, allow it to cool.

Ratatouille Tart

Ingredients:

For the crust:

- 1 ½ cups all-purpose flour
- ½ teaspoon salt
- ½ cup cold unsalted butter, cubed
- 4-5 tablespoons ice water

For the filling:

- 2 tablespoons olive oil
- 1 onion, diced
- 2 cloves garlic, minced
- 1 eggplant, diced
- 2 zucchinis, diced
- 2 red bell peppers, diced
- 4 tomatoes, diced
- Salt and pepper to taste
- 1 teaspoon dried oregano
- 1 teaspoon paprika

- ½ cup grated Manchego cheese

Instructions:

1. In a bowl, combine flour and salt to make the crust. Cut in the butter until the mixture resembles coarse crumbs. Using a fork, gradually toss in the ice water until the dough comes together. Press into a disk, cover with plastic wrap, and chill for at least half an hour.
2. Set oven temperature to 190°C/375°F.
3. Heat the olive oil in a skillet over medium heat. Sauté the garlic and onions until they are tender.
4. Include bell peppers, zucchini, and eggplant. Sauté the veggies until they are soft.
5. Add tomatoes, paprika, oregano, salt, and pepper. Cook for 5 to 7 more minutes.
6. Using a floured surface, roll out the chilled dough and place it in a tart pan. After pressing the dough into the pan, trim the edges.
7. Evenly distribute the vegetable mixture onto the crust. Add some grated Manchego cheese on top.
8. Bake for 25 to 30 minutes or until the filling is bubbling and the crust is golden brown.
9. Prior to slicing and serving, allow it to cool slightly.

Mallorcan Sweet and Savory Pastry

Ingredients:

- 4 cups all-purpose flour
- ½ cup sugar
- 1 tablespoon active dry yeast
- ½ cup warm milk
- 3 eggs

- ½ cup unsalted butter, softened
- Powdered sugar for dusting

Instructions:

1. Mix the sugar and flour in a bowl. Dissolve the yeast in warm milk and let stand until foamy, about 5 minutes.
2. Spoon the yeast mixture into the well created in the middle of the flour mixture. Add butter and eggs. Stir to produce a soft dough.
3. Until the dough is smooth and elastic, knead it for ten to fifteen minutes on a floured surface. After the dough has doubled in size, put it in a basin that has been oiled, cover it, and let it rise in a warm location for one to two hours.
4. Divide the dough into little pieces by pressing it down. Create a long rope out of each part and twist it into a spiral pattern.
5. Arrange the spirals on a parchment-lined baking sheet. Cover and let them rise for another 30 to 45 minutes.
6. Set oven temperature to 175°C/350°F.
7. Bake the ensaimadas until they are golden brown, 15 to 20 minutes.
8. Before serving, let them cool somewhat and then sprinkle with powdered sugar.

Omelette Skewers

Ingredients:

- 1 Tortilla Española (prepared according to the previous recipe)
- Cherry tomatoes
- Green olives
- Toothpicks

Instructions:

1. Chop the Tortilla Española into small square pieces.
2. Thread each toothpick with a tortilla square, a cherry tomato, and a green olive.
3. Arrange the skewers as a snack or appetizer on a serving dish.

Asturian Stuffed Bread Rolls

Ingredients:

For the dough:

- 4 cups all-purpose flour
- 1 tablespoon active dry yeast
- 1 teaspoon salt
- 1 tablespoon sugar
- 1 cup warm milk
- ½ cup unsalted butter, melted

For the filling:

- 8 slices of cooked ham
- 8 slices of Spanish chorizo

For the glaze:

- 1 egg, beaten

Instructions:

1. Combine flour, sugar, yeast, and salt in a bowl. Pour melted butter and warm milk into the center well that has been created. Stir to produce a soft dough.
2. Until the dough is smooth and elastic, knead it for five to seven minutes on a floured surface. After the dough has

doubled in size, put it in a basin that has been oiled, cover it, and let it rise in a warm location for one to two hours.

3. Divide the dough into eight equal sections by punching it down.
4. Spread each half into a circle, then arrange a chorizo and ham slice in the centre. Fold the dough over the filling and pinch the edges shut.
5. Transfer the filled rolls to a parchment-lined baking sheet. Cover and let them rise for another 30 to 45 minutes.
6. Set oven temperature to 190°C/375°F.
7. Use a beaten egg to brush the tops of the rolls.
8. Bake for golden brown, 20 to 25 minutes.
9. Before serving, allow them to cool slightly.

Sobrasada and Honey Pinwheels

Ingredients:

- 1 sheet of puff pastry
- Sobrasada (Spanish spreadable cured sausage)
- Honey

Instructions:

1. Turn the oven on to 375°F, or 190°C.
2. On a surface dusted with flour, roll out the puff pastry sheet.
3. Drizzle a small amount of sobrasada onto the puff pastry.
4. Evenly drizzle the sobrasada with honey.
5. Strictly roll the puff pastry from end to end.
6. Slice the roll, keeping the thickness at roughly 1/2 inch.
7. Arrange the pinwheels on a parchment paper-lined baking sheet.

8. Bake for 15 to 20 minutes, or until golden brown, in a preheated oven.
9. Before serving, allow it to cool somewhat.

Pan de Aceitunas (Olive Bread)

Ingredients:

- 500g bread flour
- 10g salt
- 7g instant yeast
- 350ml warm water
- 200g green olives, pitted and chopped
- 2 tablespoons olive oil

Instructions:

1. Place the flour, yeast, and salt in a large mixing basin.
2. Stirring constantly, gradually add the warm water until a dough forms.
3. Until the dough is smooth and elastic, knead it for ten minutes on a floured surface.
4. After the dough has doubled in size, please place it in a lightly oiled bowl, cover it with a fresh kitchen towel, and let it rise in a warm location for about an hour.
5. Set oven temperature to 220°C, or 425°F.
6. Gently press down on the dough and work in the chopped olives until they are thoroughly mixed throughout.
7. Form the dough into a loaf and put it on a parchment paper-lined baking pan.
8. Apply olive oil to the loaf's top.
9. Bake for 25 to 30 minutes in a preheated oven or until the bread is golden brown and hollow to the touch.
10. Before slicing and serving, allow it to cool.

Catalan Bean Salad Tart

Ingredients:

- 1 sheet of puff pastry
- 1 cup cooked white beans (such as cannellini or navy beans)
- 1 tomato, diced
- 1/2 red onion, thinly sliced
- 1/4 cup chopped fresh parsley
- 2 tablespoons red wine vinegar
- 2 tablespoons olive oil
- Salt and pepper to taste

Instructions:

1. Turn the oven on to 375°F, or 190°C.
2. Using a floured surface, roll out the puff pastry sheet and place it on a parchment paper-lined baking sheet.
3. Combine the cooked white beans, red wine vinegar, olive oil, chopped parsley, diced tomato, sliced red onion, and salt and pepper in a bowl.
4. Evenly cover the puff pastry with the bean salad mixture, leaving a border all the way around.
5. To make a rustic tart, fold the puff pastry edges over the filling.
6. Bake for 25 to 30 minutes, or until the pastry is crispy and golden brown, in a preheated oven.
7. Before slicing and serving, allow it to cool slightly.

Stuffed Peppers with Rice

Ingredients:

- 4 large bell peppers (any colour)
- 1 cup cooked rice
- 1/2 cup cooked black beans
- 1/2 cup corn kernels
- 1/2 cup diced tomatoes
- 1/4 cup chopped cilantro
- 1 teaspoon cumin
- 1 teaspoon chilli powder
- Salt and pepper to taste
- Shredded cheese for topping (optional)

Instructions:

1. Turn the oven on to 375°F, or 190°C.
2. Cut the bell peppers' tops off, removing the seeds and membranes.
3. Combine the cooked rice, cumin, chilli powder, black beans, corn kernels, diced tomatoes, chopped cilantro, and salt and pepper in a bowl.
4. Stuff the rice mixture inside the bell peppers, then put them in a baking tray.
5. Top each stuffed pepper with grated cheese, if desired.
6. Bake the baking dish in the preheated oven for thirty to thirty-five minutes or until the peppers are soft. Cover with foil.
7. Remove the foil and bake for five to ten more minutes or until the cheese is bubbling and melted.
8. Allow to cool down a little before serving.

Mallorcan Tomato and Pepper Flatbread

Ingredients:

- 1 sheet of pizza dough
- 2 tomatoes, thinly sliced
- 1/2 red onion, thinly sliced
- 1/2 green bell pepper, thinly sliced
- 1/2 red bell pepper, thinly sliced
- 2 tablespoons chopped fresh parsley
- 2 tablespoons olive oil
- Salt and pepper to taste

Instructions:

1. Set the oven's temperature to 425°F (220°C).
2. Using a floured surface, roll out the pizza dough and place it on a parchment paper-lined baking sheet.
3. Evenly distribute the bell pepper, tomato, and red onion slices over the pizza dough.
4. Drizzle olive oil and sprinkle chopped parsley on top of the veggies.
5. Season to taste with salt and pepper.
6. Bake for 15 to 20 minutes, or until the crust is crispy and golden brown, in a preheated oven.
7. Before slicing and serving, allow it to cool slightly.

Basque Custard Cake

Ingredients:

For the pastry:

- 200g all-purpose flour
- 100g unsalted butter, cold and diced

- 1 egg
- Pinch of salt

For the custard filling:

- 500ml whole milk
- 4 egg yolks
- 100g sugar
- 50g cornstarch
- 1 teaspoon vanilla extract
- Powdered sugar for dusting

Instructions:

1. Turn the oven on to 375°F, or 190°C.
2. In a food processor, combine flour, cold diced butter, egg, and salt to make the dough. Pulse until the mixture resembles coarse breadcrumbs.
3. Place the pastry on a floured board and give it a quick knead until it forms a smooth ball.
4. Refrigerate the pastry for at least 30 minutes after wrapping it in plastic wrap.
5. Using a floured surface, roll out two-thirds of the pastry to line a tart tin that has been oiled.
6. Use a fork to prick the pastry's bottom, then bake it for 10 to 12 minutes or until it's just beginning to brown.
7. Bring the milk to a near-boil in a saucepan to make the custard filling.
8. Beat the egg yolks, sugar, cornstarch, and vanilla extract together until smooth in another basin.
9. Whisk continuously as you gradually add the heated milk to the egg mixture.
10. Transfer the mixture back to the saucepan and whisk continuously over medium heat until the liquid thickens.

11. Fill the partially baked pastry shell with the custard filling.
12. Using the remaining pastry, roll it out and top the custard filling, making sure the borders are sealed tightly.
13. Bake for 25 to 30 minutes, or until the pastry is golden brown, in a preheated oven.
14. Let cool before serving and sprinkling with powdered sugar.

Ham and Cheese Croquettes

Ingredients:

- 2 tablespoons butter
- 2 tablespoons all-purpose flour
- 1 cup milk
- 100g cooked ham, finely chopped
- 100g cheese (such as Manchego or Cheddar), grated
- Salt and pepper to taste
- 1 egg, beaten
- Breadcrumbs
- Vegetable oil for frying

Instructions:

1. Melt the butter in a pot over a medium heat.
2. Cook for one to two minutes after adding the flour to make a roux.
3. Add the milk gradually and whisk until smooth.
4. Cook the mixture, stirring regularly, until it thickens.
5. Turn off the heat and thoroughly mix in the grated cheese and sliced ham.
6. Season to taste with salt and pepper.

7. Pour the mixture onto a shallow dish and chill it until it solidifies.
8. Form the mixture into little croquettes after it has solidified.
9. Coat each croquette in breadcrumbs after dipping it into the beaten egg.
10. Preheat 350°F (175°C) vegetable oil in a deep fryer or large saucepan.
11. Fry the croquettes in batches for two to three minutes or until crispy and golden brown.
12. Please take out the oil and place it on paper towels to drain.
13. Serve hot, with your choice of dipping sauce, if desired.

CHAPTER - 15
SEASONAL SENSATIONS

Springtime Orange Blossom Cake

Ingredients:

- 2 cups all-purpose flour
- 1 1/2 teaspoons baking powder
- 1/4 teaspoon salt
- 1/2 cup unsalted butter, softened
- 1 cup granulated sugar
- 2 large eggs
- 1 teaspoon vanilla extract
- 1/2 cup milk
- Zest of 1 orange
- 1 tablespoon orange blossom water

Instructions:

1. Set the oven temperature to 175°C or 350°F. Butter and dust a 9-inch circular cake pan.
2. Combine the flour, baking powder, and salt in a medium-sized bowl.
3. Cream the butter and sugar in a separate, big basin until light and creamy. Add orange zest, orange blossom water, and vanilla essence, and beat in the eggs one at a time.
4. Add the dry ingredients gradually, alternating with the milk, until just combined.
5. Fill the pan with the batter, and bake for 25 to 30 minutes, or until a toothpick inserted in the centre comes out clean.
6. After the cake has cooled in the pan for ten minutes, move it to a wire rack to finish cooling before slicing.

Summer Berry Empanadas

Ingredients:

- 2 cups all-purpose flour
- 1/4 teaspoon salt
- 1/2 cup unsalted butter, cold and cubed
- 1/4 cup cold water
- 2 cups mixed berries (such as strawberries, blueberries, and raspberries)
- 1/4 cup granulated sugar
- 1 tablespoon cornstarch
- 1 tablespoon lemon juice
- 1 egg, beaten (for egg wash)
- Granulated sugar for sprinkling

Instructions:

1. Whisk the flour and salt together in a large bowl. Cut in the cold butter until the mixture resembles coarse crumbs. Gradually add the cold water while mixing until the dough comes together.
2. Split the dough into eight equal pieces, then roll each into a ball. Each ball should be flattened into a disk, covered with plastic wrap, and chilled for half an hour.
3. Combine the mixed berries, sugar, cornstarch, and lemon juice in another basin and toss until thoroughly blended.
4. Turn the oven on to 375°F, or 190°C. Use parchment paper to line a baking sheet.
5. Create a circle out of each dough disk. Leaving a border around the edges, place a spoonful of the berry mixture onto one side of each circular. Using a fork, seal the edges of the half-moon-shaped dough formed by folding it over the filling.
6. Place the empanadas on the prepared baking sheet. Sprinkle with granulated sugar and brush the tops with a beaten egg.
7. Bake until golden brown, 20 to 25 minutes. Let cool somewhat before arranging to serve.

Autumnal Pumpkin Spice Churros

Ingredients:

- 1 cup water
- 2 tablespoons granulated sugar
- 1/2 teaspoon salt
- 2 tablespoons vegetable oil
- 1 cup all-purpose flour
- 1 teaspoon pumpkin pie spice

- Vegetable oil for frying
- 1/2 cup granulated sugar
- 1 teaspoon ground cinnamon

Instructions:

1. Put the vegetable oil, sugar, salt, and water in a saucepan. Heat to a boil in a medium setting.
2. Turn off the fire and whisk in the flour and pumpkin pie spice until a ball forms.
3. Preheat a big pot or deep fryer to 375°F (190°C) using vegetable oil.
4. Spoon the dough into a piping bag and insert a star tip into it.
5. Using scissors, cut 4-inch dough strips as you pipe them into the heated oil. Fry for 2 to 3 minutes on each side or until golden brown. Blot with paper towels.
6. Put sugar and cinnamon in a small dish. Coat the warm churros by rolling them in the sugar mixture.
7. Present right away.

Winter Citrus Olive Oil Cookies

Ingredients:

- 1/2 cup olive oil
- 3/4 cup granulated sugar
- 1 large egg
- Zest of 1 orange
- Zest of 1 lemon
- 1 teaspoon vanilla extract
- 1 3/4 cups all-purpose flour
- 1/2 teaspoon baking powder
- 1/4 teaspoon salt

Instructions:

1. Set the oven temperature to 175°C or 350°F. Use parchment paper to line a baking sheet.
2. Combine sugar and olive oil in a big basin and whisk until thoroughly mixed. Add the egg, vanilla essence, and zest from the orange and lemon and beat.
3. Combine the flour, baking powder, and salt in another bowl. Mix until a dough forms, then gradually add the dry ingredients to the wet ones.
4. Using tablespoons of dough, form balls and arrange them on the preheated baking sheet. Each ball should be flattened with a glass's bottom.
5. Bake the edges for a light golden colour, 10 to 12 minutes.
6. After the cookies have cooled for five minutes on the baking sheet, move them to a wire rack to finish cooling. Have fun!

Spring Strawberry Rhubarb Galette

Ingredients:

- 1 refrigerated pie crust (or homemade)
- 1 1/2 cups sliced strawberries
- 1 1/2 cups sliced rhubarb
- 1/4 cup granulated sugar
- 2 tablespoons cornstarch
- Zest of 1 lemon
- 1 tablespoon lemon juice
- 1 egg, beaten (for egg wash)
- Turbinado sugar for sprinkling

Instructions:

1. Set the oven temperature to 375°F, or 190°C. Use parchment paper to line a baking sheet.
2. Put the strawberries, rhubarb, cornstarch, granulated sugar, lemon zest, and lemon juice in a big bowl. Toss to coat thoroughly.
3. Roll out the pie crust using the prepared baking sheet. Scoop the strawberry-rhubarb mixture into the centre of the crust, leaving a border around the edges.
4. Fold the crust's edges over the filling, making pleats as necessary. After brushing the crust's edges with beaten egg, dust them with turbinado sugar.
5. Bake for 25 to 30 minutes or until the filling is bubbling and the crust is golden brown.
6. Before serving, let the galette cool somewhat. Heat or serve at room temperature.

Summer Peach Almond Tart

Ingredients:

- 1 refrigerated pie crust (or homemade)
- 4 ripe peaches, sliced
- 1/4 cup almond meal
- 1/4 cup granulated sugar
- 1 tablespoon all-purpose flour
- 1/2 teaspoon almond extract
- 1 egg, beaten (for egg wash)
- Sliced almonds for topping

Instructions:

1. Set the oven temperature to 375°F, or 190°C. Use parchment paper to line a baking sheet.

2. On the prepared baking sheet, roll out the pie dough.
3. Combine flour, almond extract, granulated sugar, and almond meal in a bowl.
4. Evenly cover the crust with the almond mixture, leaving a border all the way around.
5. Place the peach slices on top of the combination of almonds.
6. Fold the crust's edges over the filling, making pleats as necessary. Apply beaten egg to the crust's edges.
7. Garnish the tart's top with sliced almonds.
8. Bake for 25 to 30 minutes or until the peaches are soft and the crust is golden brown.
9. Before serving, let the tart cool somewhat.

Autumn Fig and Honey Croissants

Ingredients:

- 1 sheet puff pastry, thawed
- 6 ripe figs, sliced
- 2 tablespoons honey
- 1/4 cup chopped walnuts
- 1 egg, beaten (for egg wash)
- Powdered sugar for dusting

Instructions:

1. Set the oven temperature to 375°F, or 190°C. Use parchment paper to line a baking sheet.
2. The puff pastry should be rolled out on a board dusted with flour. Divide into rectangles.
3. Arrange the fig slices on each rectangle, then top with chopped walnuts and honey.
4. For each rectangle into a croissant by rolling it up.

5. Arrange the croissants on the ready baking sheet. Apply beaten egg as a brush.
6. Bake until golden brown, 15 to 20 minutes.
7. Before dusting the croissants with powdered sugar, let them cool slightly. Warm up and serve.

Winter Spiced Hot Chocolate Conchas

Ingredients:

For the dough:

- 2 1/4 teaspoons active dry yeast
- 1/4 cup warm water
- 1/2 cup warm milk
- 1/3 cup granulated sugar
- 1/3 cup unsalted butter, melted
- 1 teaspoon vanilla extract
- 1/2 teaspoon salt
- 1 large egg
- 3 1/2 cups all-purpose flour

For the topping:

- 1/2 cup unsalted butter, softened
- 1/2 cup granulated sugar
- 1/2 cup all-purpose flour
- 1 teaspoon ground cinnamon
- 1/2 teaspoon ground nutmeg
- 1/4 teaspoon ground cloves
- 1/4 teaspoon ground allspice
- 1/2 teaspoon vanilla extract
- Food coloring (optional)

Instructions:

1. Dissolve yeast in warm water in a small basin. Wait five minutes for it to get frothy.
2. Place the heated milk, sugar, melted butter, vanilla essence, salt, egg, and yeast mixture in a big basin. Add flour gradually until a soft dough forms.
3. Knead the dough for approximately five minutes on a surface dusted with flour until it is smooth and elastic. After the dough has doubled in size, put it in an oiled bowl, cover it, and let it rise in a warm location for an hour.
4. As you wait, prepare the topping. Beat sugar and melted butter together in a bowl until frothy and light. Mix in flour, nutmeg, cloves, allspice, ground cinnamon, and vanilla essence. Blend until thoroughly blended. If you'd like, split the topping and give each piece a dash of food colouring.
5. Set the oven temperature to 175°C or 350°F. Use parchment paper to line a baking sheet.
6. Divide the risen dough into equal halves by punching it down. Make a ball out of each part.
7. Form each ball into a flat disc. After the baking sheet is ready, place the discs on it.
8. Place the topping on top of each dough disc after scoring it into the shape of a shell with a knife or pastry cutter.
9. Bake the conchas until they are just beginning to turn golden, 15 to 20 minutes.
10. Before serving, let the conchas cool on a wire rack. Savour while sipping hot cocoa!

Springtime Lemon Lavender Madeleines

Ingredients:

- 2/3 cup all-purpose flour
- 1/2 teaspoon baking powder
- Pinch of salt
- 2 large eggs
- 1/2 cup granulated sugar
- Zest of 1 lemon
- 1 tablespoon fresh lemon juice
- 1 teaspoon dried culinary lavender flowers, finely chopped
- 1/2 cup unsalted butter, melted and cooled
- Powdered sugar for dusting

Instructions:

1. Set the oven temperature to 375°F, or 190°C—grease and dust moulds for madeleines.
2. Combine the flour, baking powder, and salt in a small bowl.
3. Beat eggs and powdered sugar together in another basin until light and frothy.
4. Add chopped lavender, lemon juice, and zest.
5. Fold in the flour mixture little by little until just incorporated.
6. Until smooth, gently fold in melted butter.
7. Transfer the batter, filling each madeleine mould to about 3/4 of the way to the top.
8. Bake the madeleines for ten to twelve minutes or until they are brown and pliable to the touch.

9. Take them out of the oven and allow them to cool in the moulds for a few minutes, then place them on a wire rack to finish cooling.
10. Before serving, dust with powdered sugar. Savour these sweet snacks with coffee or tea.

Summer Tomato Basil Focaccia

Ingredients:

- 1 1/2 cups warm water
- 2 1/4 teaspoons active dry yeast
- 1 tablespoon granulated sugar
- 4 cups all-purpose flour
- 2 teaspoons salt
- 1/4 cup extra virgin olive oil, plus more for drizzling
- 2-3 ripe tomatoes, sliced
- Handful of fresh basil leaves
- Coarse sea salt for sprinkling

Instructions:

1. Combine sugar, yeast, and warm water in a small basin. Stir until frothy, then let it sit for five to ten minutes.
2. Combine the flour and salt in a sizable mixing dish. Pour the olive oil and yeast mixture into the centre well that has been created.
3. Stir the dough until it becomes shaggy. Place the dough on a surface dusted with flour and knead it for approximately five minutes or until it becomes elastic and smooth.
4. After the dough has doubled in size, please place it in a greased bowl, cover it with a fresh kitchen towel, and let it rise in a warm location for about an hour.

5. Set the oven temperature to 200°C or 400°F. Line or grease a baking sheet with parchment paper.
6. Gently press the risen dough down and place it on the ready baking sheet. To fit the pan, gently press and stretch the dough.
7. Top the dough with tomato slices and basil leaves. Sprinkle with coarse sea salt and drizzle with a bit more olive oil.
8. Bake the focaccia for 20 to 25 minutes or until cooked through and golden brown.
9. Prior to slicing and serving, allow it to cool slightly. Savour this aromatic focaccia as an appetizer or side dish.

Autumnal Apple Cinnamon Rosettes

Ingredients:

- 2 large apples (such as Granny Smith), cored and thinly sliced
- 1 tablespoon lemon juice
- 1/4 cup granulated sugar
- 1 tablespoon ground cinnamon
- 1 sheet puff pastry, thawed
- Powdered sugar for dusting

Instructions:

1. Set the oven temperature to 375°F, or 190°C. Oil a muffin pan.
2. Toss apple slices with cinnamon, granulated sugar, and lemon juice in a bowl until thoroughly coated.
3. Using a surface dusted with flour, roll out the puff pastry to form a sizable rectangle.
4. Slice the pastry into slender, two-inch-wide strips.

5. Slightly overlap the apple slices as you arrange them along the length of each pastry strip.
6. Place each pastry strip in the muffin tin that has been prepared after rolling it into a rosette.
7. Bake for 25 to 30 minutes or until the apples are soft and the pastry is golden brown.
8. After a few minutes, let the rosettes cool in the pan before moving them to a wire rack to finish cooling.
9. Before serving, dust with powdered sugar. Savour these sophisticated apple cinnamon rosettes as a delicious fall dessert.

Winter Chestnut Chocolate Truffles

Ingredients:

- 1 cup roasted chestnuts, peeled
- 1/4 cup unsweetened cocoa powder
- 1/4 cup powdered sugar
- 1/4 teaspoon vanilla extract
- Pinch of salt
- 2-3 tablespoons heavy cream
- Cocoa powder, crushed nuts, or shredded coconut for coating (optional)

Instructions:

1. Pulse roasted chestnuts in a food processor until finely ground.
2. Include salt, vanilla essence, powdered sugar, and chocolate powder. Pulse until thoroughly mixed.
3. Add the heavy cream gradually, one tablespoon at a time, and pulse the ingredients to produce a smooth dough.

4. Using a rolling pin, roll the dough into tiny balls and arrange on a parchment paper-lined baking sheet.
5. You can coat the truffles with cocoa powder, chopped almonds, or shredded coconut if you'd like.
6. Refrigerate the truffles for a minimum of half an hour or until they solidify.
7. As a winter treat or gift, serve these rich and decadent chestnut chocolate truffles chilled.

Springtime Almond Orange Blossom Biscotti

Ingredients:

- 1/2 cup unsalted butter, softened
- 3/4 cup granulated sugar
- 2 large eggs
- 1 teaspoon almond extract
- Zest of 1 orange
- 2 cups all-purpose flour
- 1 teaspoon baking powder
- 1/4 teaspoon salt
- 1/2 cup sliced almonds

Instructions:

1. Set the oven temperature to 175°C or 350°F. Use parchment paper to line a baking sheet.
2. Using a big bowl, beat melted butter and powdered sugar until frothy and light.
3. Add the orange zest and almond extract after beating in the eggs one at a time.

4. Combine the flour, baking powder, and salt in another basin. Mixing until a dough forms, gradually add the dry ingredients to the wet ones.
5. Until the almond slices are appropriately distributed throughout the dough, fold them in.
6. Split the dough in two. Form each part into a log that is roughly 2 inches broad and 12 inches long. Spread out the logs on the baking sheet that has been prepared.
7. Bake the logs for 25 to 30 minutes or until they are firm to the touch and have a light golden colour.
8. Take the logs out of the oven and allow them to cool for ten minutes on the baking sheet.
9. Lower the oven's setting to 325°F, or 160°C. After moving the logs to a chopping block, cut them into 1/2-inch-thick slices using a diagonal cut.
10. Transfer the biscotti to the baking sheet, cut side down, and bake for a further 10 to 15 minutes or until golden and crisp.
11. Before serving, let the biscotti cool thoroughly on wire racks. Savour these crispy almond-flavoured orange blossom biscotti while sipping your coffee or tea.

Summer Cornbread Muffins with Jalapeño

Ingredients:

- 1 cup yellow cornmeal
- 1 cup all-purpose flour
- 1/4 cup granulated sugar
- 1 tablespoon baking powder
- 1/2 teaspoon salt
- 1 cup milk
- 1/4 cup unsalted butter, melted
- 2 large eggs

- 1 cup fresh or canned corn kernels
- 1 jalapeño pepper, seeded and finely chopped

Instructions:

1. Set the oven temperature to 200°C or 400°F. Use paper liners to line a muffin tray.
2. Combine cornmeal, flour, sugar, baking powder, and salt in a sizable bowl.
3. In another dish, thoroughly whisk together the eggs, melted butter, and milk.
4. Add the wet mixture to the dry mixture and whisk just until blended. Add chopped jalapeño and corn kernels and mix well.
5. Evenly distribute the batter into each muffin cup, filling it to about 3/4 of the way.
6. Bake for 15 to 18 minutes, or until a toothpick inserted into the centre of the muffins comes out clean and the muffins are golden brown.
7. Take the muffins out of the oven and allow them to rest in the pan for five minutes. Then, place them on a wire rack to finish cooling.
8. Serve these tasty muffins warm out of the oven or at room temperature. They go well with soups or barbecued foods.

Autumnal Pear Frangipane Tartlets

Ingredients:

For the pastry:

- 1 1/4 cups all-purpose flour
- 1/4 cup granulated sugar
- 1/2 cup unsalted butter, cold and cubed

- 1 egg yolk
- 1-2 tablespoons ice water

For the frangipane filling:

- 1/2 cup almond meal
- 1/4 cup granulated sugar
- 1 egg
- 1/2 teaspoon almond extract
- 2 ripe pears, thinly sliced
- 2 tablespoons apricot jam, warmed (for glazing)

Instructions:

1. To make the pastry, pulse the flour and sugar in a food processor. Process the mixture until it resembles coarse crumbs after adding the cold butter. One tablespoon at a time, add the egg yolk and ice water, pulsing until the dough comes together.
2. Place the dough on a lightly floured surface and give it a quick knead until it's smooth. After flattening it into a disk, cover it with plastic wrap and chill it for a minimum of half an hour.
3. Set the oven temperature to 375°F, or 190°C. Oil a small tart pan.
4. To make the frangipane filling, combine almond meal, sugar, egg, and almond extract in a bowl and stir until well combined.
5. Using a surface dusted with flour, roll out the cold pastry dough. To fit the tiny tart pan, cut out circles, then press them into the moulds.
6. Fill each tart shell with frangipane filling. Arrange pear slices in a pretty pattern on top.

7. Bake for twenty to twenty-five minutes or until the filling is set and the pastry is golden.
8. Take them out of the oven, then drizzle some hot apricot jam over the pear slices to give them a glossy look.
9. After a few minutes, let the tartlets cool in the pan before moving them to a wire rack to finish cooling.
10. As a beautiful fall dessert, serve these adorable pear frangipane tartlets.

CHAPTER - 16
PORTABLE SPANISH BAKES FOR OUTDOOR DINING

Tortilla Espanola Muffins

Ingredients:

- 4 large eggs
- 2 medium potatoes, peeled and thinly sliced
- 1/2 onion, thinly sliced
- Salt and pepper to taste
- Olive oil for frying

Instructions:

1. Grease a muffin tin with olive oil and preheat the oven to 350°F (175°C).
2. Preheat olive oil in a skillet over medium heat. Add the onions and potatoes and cut thinly. Season with pepper and salt. Simmer the potatoes for 8 to 10 minutes or until they are soft and starting to colour.

3. Beat the eggs in a mixing dish and then stir in the cooked potato and onion mixture. Mix thoroughly until fully incorporated.
4. Fill each muffin tray about 3/4 of the way to the top with the egg and potato mixture.
5. Bake for 15 to 20 minutes, or until the muffins are set and have a light golden colour on top, in a preheated oven.
6. Before taking the muffins out of the tray, let them cool slightly. Heat or serve at room temperature.

Empanada Gallega Picnic Pies

Ingredients:

- 2 sheets of store-bought puff pastry, thawed
- 1 can (6 ounces) tuna, drained
- 1/2 onion, finely chopped
- 1/2 red bell pepper, finely chopped
- 1 hard-boiled egg, chopped
- 1/4 cup green olives, sliced
- Salt and pepper to taste
- Egg wash (1 egg beaten with 1 tablespoon of water)

Instructions:

1. Preheat the oven to 375°F (190°C) and place parchment paper on a baking pan.
2. Put the tuna, red bell pepper, onion, chopped hard-boiled egg, and sliced green olives in a mixing dish. Season with salt and pepper to taste.
3. Roll out a single puff pastry sheet on a surface dusted with flour. Transfer to the prepared baking sheet.
4. Evenly cover the puff pastry with the tuna filling, leaving a thin border all the way around.

5. Cover the filling with the second layer of puff pastry that you have rolled out. Press the edges together to seal.
6. Apply the egg wash to the pastry's top.
7. To let steam out of the pastry, cut tiny slits on the top with a sharp knife.
8. Bake for 25 to 30 minutes, or until the pastry is crisp and golden brown, in a preheated oven.
9. Before slicing and serving, let the empanada gallega to cool slightly.

Pan con Tomate Roll-ups

Ingredients:

- 4 slices of crusty bread
- 2 ripe tomatoes, halved
- 2 cloves garlic, peeled
- Extra virgin olive oil
- Salt to taste
- Serrano ham or prosciutto

Instructions:

1. Set the broiler or grill to high heat.
2. Toast the crusty bread slices until they are golden brown on all sides.
3. Gently rub the tomato halves' cut sides over the toasted bread, pressing down to transfer the pulp and liquids to the bread.
4. To add flavour, rub the garlic cloves over the bread that has been smeared with tomato paste.
5. Sprinkle salt to taste and drizzle extra virgin olive oil over each slice.

6. Top each slice of bread with a slice of prosciutto or Serrano ham.
7. Tightly roll up each slice, and if needed, fasten it with toothpicks.
8. For outdoor eating, cover the pan con tomate roll-ups snugly in foil and serve immediately.

Churro Bites with Chocolate Dipping Sauce

Ingredients:

- 1 cup water
- 2 tablespoons white sugar
- 1/2 teaspoon salt
- 2 tablespoons vegetable oil
- 1 cup all-purpose flour
- 1/4 cup sugar mixed with 1 teaspoon ground cinnamon
- Vegetable oil for frying
- 4 ounces dark chocolate, chopped
- 1/2 cup heavy cream

Instructions:

1. Put water, salt, two teaspoons of sugar, and two tablespoons of vegetable oil in a pot. Heat to a boil in a medium setting.
2. Turn off the fire and whisk in the flour until a ball forms.
3. Preheat a big pot or deep fryer to 375°F (190°C) for frying vegetables.
4. Transfer dough into a piping bag and insert a star tip into it.

5. Using kitchen scissors, cut 1-inch strips of dough into the required length by piping them into the heated oil. When golden, fry and then drain on paper towels.
6. Combine cinnamon and 1/4 cup sugar. Dredge the drained churros in a combination of sugar and cinnamon.
7. Bring heavy cream to a simmer for the chocolate dipping sauce. After adding the chocolate chips, wait two minutes. Mix until creamy and smooth.
8. Present warm churro nibbles accompanied by a chocolate dip sauce.

Spanish Potato and Onion Frittata Squares

Ingredients:

- 4 tablespoons olive oil
- 2 large potatoes, peeled and thinly sliced
- 1 onion, thinly sliced
- 8 eggs
- Salt and pepper to taste
- 1/4 cup grated Manchego cheese
- 2 tablespoons chopped fresh parsley

Instructions:

1. Set oven temperature to 175°C/350°F.
2. In a large ovenproof skillet, heat the olive oil over medium heat. Add the potatoes and onions, and cook and stir for ten minutes or until the potatoes are soft and the onions are transparent.
3. Beat the eggs, salt, and pepper in a basin. Pour the egg mixture over the potatoes and onions in the skillet. Gently mix everything.

4. Cook without stirring for about five minutes or until the edges are firm. Sprinkle with some shredded Manchego cheese.
5. Place the pan in the preheated oven and bake for 10 to 12 minutes, or until the eggs are set and the cheese is bubbling.
6. Take it out of the oven and allow it to cool slightly. Once the parsley is chopped, sprinkle and cut into squares. Heat or serve at room temperature.

Tarta de Santiago Energy Bars

Ingredients:

- 1 cup almonds
- 1 cup pitted dates
- 1/4 cup honey
- 1 teaspoon ground cinnamon
- Zest of 1 lemon
- Pinch of salt
- Powdered sugar (optional for dusting)

Instructions:

1. Set oven temperature to 175°C/350°F. Place parchment paper into a baking dish.
2. Arrange almonds on a baking sheet and toast them for 8 to 10 minutes in a preheated oven or until they become aromatic and lightly golden. Allow to cool.
3. Place the pitted dates, honey, cinnamon, lemon zest, toasted almonds, and a small amount of salt in a food processor. Pulse just until the mixture forms a sticky dough and comes together.

4. Evenly and firmly press the mixture into the baking dish that has been prepared.
5. Bake for 15 to 20 minutes, or until the edges are golden brown, in a preheated oven.
6. Allow to cool fully before cutting into bars. If desired, dust with powdered sugar.

Olive and Herb Focaccia Loaves

Ingredients:

- 1 1/2 cups warm water
- 1 tablespoon honey
- 2 1/4 teaspoons active dry yeast
- 4 cups all-purpose flour
- 1/4 cup extra virgin olive oil, plus more for drizzling
- 1 teaspoon salt
- 1 cup pitted olives, chopped
- 2 tablespoons fresh rosemary, chopped
- Coarse sea salt for sprinkling

Instructions:

1. Place the yeast, honey, and warm water in a sizable mixing dish. Let it remain until frothy, about 5 to 10 minutes.
2. Include salt, flour, and olive oil in the yeast mixture. Stir to form a dough.
3. Place the dough on a floured area and knead it for five to seven minutes or until it becomes elastic and smooth.
4. After the dough has been oiled and covered with a fresh kitchen towel, let it rise in a warm location for approximately one hour or until it has doubled in size.

5. Set oven temperature to 200°C/400°F. After the dough has risen, punch it down and split it in half.
6. Roll each portion into a rectangle and place on a parchment paper-lined baking pan.
7. Press freshly chopped rosemary and olives into the dough's tops.
8. Sprinkle coarse sea salt and drizzle olive oil over each loaf.
9. Bake for 20 to 25 minutes, or until cooked through and golden brown, in a preheated oven.
10. Before slicing and serving, allow it to cool slightly.

Piquillo Pepper and Goat Cheese Empanadas

Ingredients:

- 1 package (2 sheets) of store-bought puff pastry, thawed
- 4 ounces goat cheese
- 1/2 cup piquillo peppers, chopped
- 1 egg, beaten (for egg wash)
- Fresh parsley, chopped (optional, for garnish)

Instructions:

1. Set oven temperature to 190°C/375°F. Use parchment paper to line a baking sheet.
2. Using a surface dusted with flour, roll out the puff pastry and cut it into squares.
3. Combine chopped piquillo peppers and goat cheese in a small bowl.
4. Top each pastry square with a dollop of the goat cheese mixture.

5. Fold the dough over the filling to create a triangular shape, then crimp the corners with a fork to seal them.
6. Use a beaten egg to brush the empanadas' tops lightly.
7. Transfer the empanadas to the prepared baking sheet and bake for 15 to 20 minutes, or until puffed and golden brown, in a preheated oven.
8. Before serving, garnish with freshly chopped parsley, if preferred.

Patatas Bravas Hand Pies

Ingredients:

- 2 sheets puff pastry, thawed
- 2 large potatoes, peeled and diced
- 1/2 onion, finely chopped
- 2 cloves garlic, minced
- 1/4 cup tomato sauce
- 1 teaspoon smoked paprika
- 1/2 teaspoon chilli powder (adjust to taste)
- Salt and pepper to taste
- Olive oil for frying
- 1 egg, beaten (for egg wash)

Instructions:

1. Set oven temperature to 200°C/400°F. Use parchment paper to line a baking sheet.
2. Heat the olive oil in a large skillet over medium heat. Add the diced potatoes and cook for ten minutes or until they are soft and golden brown.
3. Combine the potatoes in a skillet with the chopped onion and minced garlic. Cook for about 5 minutes or until the onion is softened.

4. Mix in the chilli powder, tomato sauce, smoked paprika, salt, and pepper. Simmer for two to three more minutes. Remove the mixture from the heat and allow it to cool somewhat.
5. Using a surface dusted with flour, roll out the puff pastry. Divide into squares.
6. Top each pastry square with a small amount of the potato mixture.
7. Fold the dough over the filling to create a triangular shape, then crimp the corners with a fork to seal them.
8. Use a beaten egg to brush the tops of the hand pies.
9. Transfer the hand pies to the prepared baking sheet and bake for 15 to 20 minutes, or until puffed and golden brown, in the preheated oven.
10. Top with your preferred dipping sauce and serve warm.

Almond and Orange Polvorones Cookies

Ingredients:

- 1 cup almond flour
- 1/2 cup powdered sugar
- Zest of 1 orange
- 1/4 teaspoon ground cinnamon
- 1/4 cup unsalted butter, softened
- 1/2 teaspoon almond extract

Instructions:

1. Set oven temperature to 175°C/350°F. Use parchment paper to line a baking sheet.
2. Place almond flour, powdered sugar, orange zest, and ground cinnamon in a mixing bowl.

3. Combine the dry ingredients with the softened butter and almond essence. Stir to form a dough.
4. Roll the dough into little balls and arrange them on the ready baking sheet.
5. Use the palm of your hand to flatten each ball softly.
6. Bake for 12 to 15 minutes, or until the sides are just beginning to turn brown, in the preheated oven.
7. After a few minutes, let the cookies cool on the baking sheet before moving them to a wire rack to finish cooling.
8. If desired, dust with more powdered sugar before serving.

Bacalao Croquettes with Garlic Aioli

Ingredients:

- 1/2 pound salted cod (bacalao)
- 2 cups milk
- 2 tablespoons unsalted butter
- 2 tablespoons all-purpose flour
- 1/4 cup finely chopped onion
- 2 cloves garlic, minced
- 1/4 teaspoon ground nutmeg
- Salt and pepper to taste
- 1 egg, beaten
- Bread crumbs for coating
- Olive oil for frying

Instructions:

1. To get rid of extra salt, rinse the salted fish under cold water. Chop into tiny fragments.

2. Put the milk and salted cod into a saucepan. After bringing to a simmer, simmer for ten minutes on medium heat.
3. Take the salted fish out of the milk and drain it well. Using a fork, flake the fish and set it aside.
4. Melt butter in a different pot over a medium heat. Add minced garlic and diced onion. Simmer for about 5 minutes or until tender.
5. Add the flour and cook, stirring frequently, for two minutes.
6. Until smooth and thickened, gradually whisk in the saved milk from boiling the salted fish.
7. Add the ground nutmeg, salt, and pepper to the pot with the flaked salted fish. Mix everything.
8. Cook for two to three more minutes, then transfer the mixture to a bowl and allow it to cool fully.
9. Form the mixture into tiny croquettes after it has cooled.
10. Coat each croquette in bread crumbs after dipping it into a beaten egg.
11. Warm the olive oil in a skillet over medium heat. Cook the croquettes until they are crispy and golden brown on all sides.
12. Present the hot bacalao croquettes with a dipping garlic aioli.

Spanish Olive Breadsticks

Ingredients:

- 1 1/2 cups all-purpose flour
- 1 teaspoon baking powder
- 1/2 teaspoon salt
- 1/4 cup olive oil
- 1/4 cup water

- 1/4 cup chopped Spanish olives
- 1 tablespoon chopped fresh rosemary
- Coarse sea salt for sprinkling

Instructions:

1. Preheat the oven to 375°F (190°C) and place parchment paper on a baking pan.
2. Combine the flour, baking powder, and salt in a mixing dish.
3. Stir the dry ingredients until a dough forms, gradually adding water and olive oil.
4. Until the fresh rosemary and chopped olives are appropriately distributed throughout the dough, fold them in.
5. Separate the dough into tiny pieces and roll each into a slender rope.
6. Arrange the ropes, leaving space between each breadstick on the baking sheet that has been prepared.
7. Use coarse sea salt to coat the breadsticks.
8. Bake for 12 to 15 minutes, or until crispy and golden brown, in a preheated oven.
9. Before serving, let the breadsticks cool somewhat. Snacken or pair with your preferred dips, enjoy!

Flan de Cafe Cupcakes

Ingredients:

- 1 1/2 cups granulated sugar divided
- 1/4 cup water
- 1 cup strong brewed coffee
- 1 cup heavy cream
- 4 large eggs

- 1 teaspoon vanilla extract
- Whipped cream and chocolate shavings for garnish (optional)

Instructions:

1. Set oven temperature to 175°C/350°F. Use paper liners to line a muffin tray.
2. Put one cup of sugar and one cup of water in a small saucepan. Stirring regularly, cook over medium heat until the sugar melts and the mixture takes on an amber hue.
3. Immediately fill each muffin cup to the brim with caramel, swirling to coat the bottom.
4. Heat the heavy cream and brewed coffee in another saucepan until it's hot but not boiling.
5. In a mixing basin, thoroughly beat eggs, vanilla extract, and the remaining 1/2 cup sugar.
6. Carefully add the heated coffee mixture to the egg mixture while continuing to whisk to avoid curdling.
7. Almost to the top, pour the custard mixture into each of the muffin cups that have been prepared.
8. After positioning the muffin tray in a bigger baking pan, fill the pan halfway up the edges of the muffin cups with hot water.
9. Bake for 30 to 35 minutes in a preheated oven or until the cupcakes are set but the centre is still somewhat jiggly.
10. Once the cupcakes have cooled to room temperature, remove the muffin pan from the water bath.
11. After cooling, place the cupcakes in the refrigerator for at least two hours or overnight.
12. To serve, flip each cupcake onto a dish after running a knife along its edge. If desired, garnish with chocolate shavings and whipped cream. Savour the smooth panna cotta cupcakes!

Pisto Stuffed Pitas

Ingredients:

- 2 tablespoons olive oil
- 1 onion, chopped
- 2 cloves garlic, minced
- 1 red bell pepper, diced
- 1 green bell pepper, diced
- 2 zucchinis, diced
- 1 can (14 ounces) diced tomatoes
- 1 teaspoon smoked paprika
- Salt and pepper to taste
- 4 whole wheat pitas
- 1/2 cup crumbled feta cheese
- Fresh parsley, chopped, for garnish

Instructions:

1. Heat the olive oil in a big skillet over medium heat. When the onion and garlic are minced and softened, add them and sauté.
2. Add diced zucchini and red and green bell peppers to the skillet. Sauté the veggies until they are soft.
3. Add the smoked paprika and diced tomatoes. Season with salt and pepper to taste. Simmer for an additional five minutes.
4. Halve the whole wheat pitas and reheat them in the oven or toaster.
5. Stuff the prepared pesto mixture into each pita half.
6. Top each filled pita half with a little bit of crumbled feta cheese.

7. Before serving, garnish with freshly cut parsley. Savour the robust and aromatic pesto-stuffed pitas as a delectable alfresco eating choice!

Spanish-Inspired Chorizo and Cheese Scones

Ingredients:

- 2 cups all-purpose flour
- 1 tablespoon baking powder
- 1/2 teaspoon salt
- 1/4 teaspoon black pepper
- 1/4 cup unsalted butter, cold and cubed
- 1/2 cup Spanish chorizo, diced
- 1 cup grated Manchego cheese
- 2/3 cup buttermilk
- 1 large egg, beaten (for egg wash)

Instructions:

1. Set the oven temperature to 200°C or 400°F. Use parchment paper to line a baking sheet.
2. Place the flour, baking powder, salt, and black pepper into a sizable mixing basin.
3. Stir the flour mixture with the cold cubed butter. Work the butter into the flour with your fingertips or a pastry cutter until it resembles coarse crumbs.
4. Add the shredded Manchego cheese and diced chorizo and stir until they are uniformly distributed.
5. Create a well in the middle of the blend and add the buttermilk. Mix until barely incorporated, taking care not to blend too much.

6. Place the dough on a lightly floured surface. Pat it gently into a circle that is one inch thick.
7. Slice the circular into eight wedges using a sharp knife.
8. Place the scones, with space between them, on the baking sheet that has been prepared.
9. Use a beaten egg to brush the scones' tops lightly.
10. Bake for 15 to 18 minutes, or until cooked through and golden brown, in a preheated oven.
11. Before serving, let the scones cool somewhat. Please take pleasure in them heated or at room temperature.

CHAPTER - 17
SPANISH HOLIDAY AND CELEBRATION BAKE RECIPES

Almond Nougat

Ingredients:

- 250g whole almonds
- 250g sugar
- 100g honey
- 1 egg white
- Wafer sheets

Instructions:

1. For ten minutes, roast the almonds at 180°C (350°F) in the oven.
2. Using a candy thermometer, heat sugar and honey in a pot until the temperature reaches 150°C (300°F).
3. Beat until stiff peaks form out of the egg white.

4. While beating the egg white, slowly pour the heated sugar mixture over it.
5. Add the toasted almonds and stir.
6. Fill a mould with the nougat mixture after lining it with wafer sheets.
7. Firmly press down and allow it to cool fully before slicing.

Shortbread Cookies

Ingredients:

- 250g all-purpose flour
- 125g lard or vegetable shortening
- 125g sugar
- 1/2 teaspoon ground cinnamon
- Zest of 1 lemon

Instructions:

1. Set the oven's temperature to 180°C (350°F).
2. Combine the flour, sugar, lemon zest, and cinnamon in a bowl.
3. Until a dough forms, mix the dry ingredients with the shortening or lard.
4. Using a rolling pin, roll the dough into tiny balls and arrange on a parchment paper-lined baking sheet.
5. Use the palm of your hand to flatten each ball softly.
6. Bake for a light golden colour, 15 to 20 minutes.
7. Before serving, let the mantecados cool fully.

Galician Meat Pie

Ingredients:

- 500g puff pastry
- 300g ground beef or pork
- 1 onion, chopped
- 2 bell peppers, diced
- 2 tomatoes, chopped
- 2 hard-boiled eggs, sliced
- Olives, pitted and sliced
- Salt and pepper to taste
- Olive oil

Instructions:

1. Set the oven's temperature to 180°C (350°F).
2. In a skillet over medium heat, sauté the bell peppers and onion until they are tender.
3. Add the ground beef and fry it until it turns brown.
4. Cook for a further five minutes after adding the chopped tomatoes.
5. After rolling out the puff pastry, put half of it on a parchment paper-lined baking sheet.
6. Cover the pastry with the meat mixture, leaving an outer border.
7. Place the olives and sliced eggs on top of the meat.
8. Seal the edges and cover with the remaining pastry.
9. Use a beaten egg to buff the top gently.
10. Bake the pastry for 30 to 35 minutes or until it turns golden brown.
11. Allow to cool somewhat before slicing and serving the empanada.

Churros with Hot Chocolate

Ingredients for churros:

- 250ml water
- 125g all-purpose flour
- 50g butter
- Pinch of salt
- Vegetable oil for frying
- Sugar for dusting

Ingredients for hot chocolate:

- 250ml milk
- 100g dark chocolate, chopped
- 1 tablespoon sugar

Instructions:

1. Bring the water, butter, and salt to a boil in a saucepan.
2. Turn off the fire and whisk in the flour just enough to produce a smooth dough.
3. Preheat the vegetable oil in a heavy-bottomed saucepan or deep fryer to 180°C (350°F).
4. Spoon the dough into a piping bag and insert a star tip into it.
5. Insert dough strips into the heated oil and cook for two to three minutes on each side or until golden brown and crispy.
6. While still warm, stir in the sugar after draining on paper towels.
7. To make the hot chocolate, place milk in a saucepan and heat it until it steams but does not boil.
8. Turn off the heat and mix in the sugar and chopped chocolate until smooth and melted.

9. Present hot chocolate for dipping alongside churros.

Spanish Creme Brulee

Ingredients:

- 500ml whole milk
- 4 egg yolks
- 100g sugar
- Zest of 1 orange
- 1 cinnamon stick
- 20g cornstarch
- Demerara sugar for caramelizing

Instructions:

1. Heat the milk, orange zest, and cinnamon stick in a skillet over medium heat until they almost boil.
2. Beat the egg yolks, sugar, and cornstarch together in a bowl until pale and creamy.
3. Whisk continuously as you gradually add the heated milk mixture to the egg mixture.
4. Transfer the mixture back to the pot and whisk continuously over low heat until it thickens.
5. Turn off the heat and pour the mixture into serving plates or ramekins through a filter.
6. Refrigerate for two hours or overnight or until set.
7. Dust each crema Catalana with a small amount of demerara sugar just before serving.
8. Use a kitchen torch or broiler to caramelize the sugar until it turns golden and bubbly.
9. Before serving, let the sugar solidify.

Spanish Honey Fritters

Ingredients:

- 500g all-purpose flour
- 100ml olive oil
- 100ml white wine
- Zest of 1 lemon
- Pinch of salt
- Vegetable oil for frying

Instructions:

1. Using a big bowl, stir together flour, salt, white wine, olive oil, and lemon zest until a dough forms.
2. Using a floured surface, knead the dough until it becomes elastic and smooth.
3. Using your hands, spread out each small ball of dough into a thin circle.
4. Preheat the vegetable oil in a heavy-bottomed saucepan or deep fryer to 180°C (350°F).
5. Fry the dough circles in batches for two to three minutes on each side or until they are crispy and golden brown.
6. Pour into paper towels and, while still warm, sprinkle with honey.
7. Present pestiños as a delicious dessert.

Spanish Saint John's Cake

Ingredients:

- 500g bread flour
- 200ml warm water
- 100ml olive oil
- 50g sugar

- 10g salt
- 25g fresh yeast
- Assorted fruits for topping (such as cherries, apricots, or figs)
- Pine nuts for topping
- Sugar for sprinkling

Instructions:

1. Add sugar and yeast to warm water, and let sit until frothy, about ten minutes.
2. Combine the flour and salt in a large bowl. Stir in the yeast mixture and olive oil.
3. Work the dough into an elastic and smooth texture. For one hour, cover it and allow it to rise.
4. Turn the oven on to 200°C, or 400°F. Roll the pastry into a narrow rectangle.
5. Place the dough on a parchment paper-lined baking pan.
6. Place the mixed fruits on top of the dough and top with sugar and pine nuts.
7. Bake until golden brown, 20 to 25 minutes. Before slicing and serving, let it cool.

Spanish Fried Green Peppers

Ingredients:

- 250g Padrón peppers
- Olive oil for frying
- Coarse sea salt for sprinkling

Instructions:

1. Rinse the Padrón peppers and use paper towels to pat dry.

2. In a large skillet over medium-high heat, warm the olive oil.
3. Add the peppers to the skillet and cook for 5 to 7 minutes or until the peppers are blistered and charred in places.
4. Move the crispy-fried peppers to a platter for presentation.
5. Before serving, sprinkle with coarse sea salt. Savour them as a tasty side dish or appetizer.

Spanish Spicy Potatoes

Ingredients:

- 500g potatoes, peeled and diced
- Olive oil for frying
- Salt to taste
- For the bravas sauce:
- 2 tablespoons olive oil
- 2 cloves garlic, minced
- 1 teaspoon smoked paprika
- 1/2 teaspoon cayenne pepper
- 250g tomato sauce
- Salt and pepper to taste

Instructions:

1. In a large skillet, heat olive oil over medium-high heat. Add the diced potatoes and fry until golden brown and crispy—season with salt and drain on paper towels.
2. In a separate saucepan, heat olive oil over medium heat. Add minced garlic, smoked paprika, and cayenne pepper. Cook for 1-2 minutes until fragrant.
3. Stir in the tomato sauce and simmer for 5-7 minutes until the sauce thickens—season with salt and pepper to taste.

4. Serve the fried potatoes with bravas sauce drizzled on top. Enjoy this classic Spanish tapa!

Spanish Garlic Shrimp

Ingredients:

- 500g large shrimp, peeled and deveined
- 6 cloves garlic, thinly sliced
- 2 dried chilli peppers (optional)
- Olive oil
- Salt and pepper to taste
- Chopped parsley for garnish

Instructions:

1. In a big skillet over medium heat, warm the olive oil. Sliced garlic and dried chile peppers, if using, should be added and cooked for one minute or until fragrant.
2. Add the shrimp to the skillet and cook for 2 to 3 minutes on each side or until they are pink and opaque.
3. Season to taste with salt and pepper.
4. Before serving, garnish with finely chopped parsley. Savour these delectable garlic shrimp as a main course or as a great snack!

Galician Style Octopus

Ingredients:

- 1 giant octopus (about 1-1.5 kg)
- 1 onion, peeled and halved
- 2 bay leaves
- Coarse sea salt
- Smoked paprika (optional)

- Olive oil

Instructions:

1. Give the octopus a thorough cleaning, making sure the beak and body are free of any debris.
2. Add the onion halves, bay leaves, and a little coarse sea salt to a large saucepan of water.
3. Bring the water to a boil over high heat. When the saucepan is boiling, carefully add the octopus.
4. Simmer the octopus on medium-low heat for 45 to 60 minutes or until it is soft. A knife or fork should glide smoothly into the thickest portion of the octopus to indicate when it is done.
5. After cooking, take the octopus out of the pot and give it a little time to cool.
6. Chop the octopus into small pieces and place it on a dish for serving.
7. Before serving, drizzle with olive oil and, if using, sprinkle with smoked paprika. Savour this classic Galician meal with some crusty bread!

Spanish Fish Escabeche

Ingredients:

- 500g firm white fish fillets (such as cod or haddock)
- All-purpose flour for dusting
- Olive oil for frying
- 1 onion, thinly sliced
- 2 carrots, thinly sliced
- 2 cloves garlic, minced
- 1 bay leaf
- 1 teaspoon whole black peppercorns

- 1 teaspoon dried oregano
- 1 teaspoon ground cumin
- 1/2 teaspoon smoked paprika
- 100ml white wine vinegar
- 100ml white wine
- Salt and pepper to taste

Instructions:

1. Lightly sprinkle the fish fillets with flour after seasoning them with salt and pepper.
2. Warm the olive oil in a large skillet over medium-high heat. Fry the fish fillets for two to three minutes on each side, or until golden brown. Remove them from the skillet and set them aside.
3. If necessary, add a little extra olive oil to the same skillet. Add the garlic, carrots, and onion and sauté until softened.
4. Fill the skillet with the smoked paprika, cumin, black peppercorns, oregano, and bay leaf. Mix everything.
5. Add the white wine and white wine vinegar, then boil.
6. Spoon the vegetable mixture over the top of the cooked fish fillets when you return them to the skillet.
7. To enable the flavours to blend, cover and simmer for five to ten minutes.
8. If desired, top the warm or cold fish escabeche with fresh herbs.

Spanish Potato Salad

Ingredients:

- 500g potatoes, peeled and diced
- 2 carrots, peeled and diced

- 150g green peas (fresh or frozen)
- 3 hard-boiled eggs, chopped
- 100g mayonnaise
- 2 tablespoons olive oil
- 1 tablespoon white wine vinegar
- Salt and pepper to taste
- Olives and canned tuna (optional, for garnish)

Instructions:

1. Cook the carrots and potatoes in salted water until they are soft. In the last five minutes of cooking, add the green peas. After draining, allow to cool.
2. Put the cooked potatoes, diced hard-boiled eggs, carrots, and green peas in a big bowl.
3. Combine the mayonnaise, white wine vinegar, and olive oil in a small bowl. Season with salt and pepper.
4. Drizzle the potato mixture with the dressing and gently toss to incorporate.
5. If preferred, garnish with olives and canned tuna.
6. Let it cool in the fridge for at least one hour before serving. Savour this light lunch or side dish of delicious Spanish potato salad!

Andalusian Cold Tomato Soup

Ingredients:

- 1 kg ripe tomatoes, chopped
- 1 cucumber, peeled and chopped
- 1 green bell pepper, chopped
- 1 small onion, chopped
- 2 cloves garlic, minced
- 50ml extra virgin olive oil

- 30ml red wine vinegar
- 1 teaspoon salt
- 1/2 teaspoon black pepper
- 2 slices stale bread, crusts removed
- Cold water, as needed
- Optional toppings: chopped cucumber, bell pepper, onion, croutons, or drizzle of olive oil

Instructions:

1. Combine the diced tomatoes, cucumber, onion, garlic, bell pepper, vinegar, olive oil, salt, and black pepper in a food processor or blender. Process until smooth.
2. Cut the stale bread into little bits and incorporate it into the blender. Repeatedly blend until the soup is smooth and the bread is well combined.
3. If the gazpacho is too thick, add a small amount of cold water at a time until it reaches the right consistency.
4. Taste and make any necessary seasoning adjustments.
5. To let the flavours mingle, chill the gazpacho in the fridge for at least two hours before serving.
6. Present the chilled gazpacho adorned with your preferred garnishes. Savour this fantastic Andalusian favourite during the summer heat!

Valencian Paella

Ingredients:

- 300g bomba or calasparra rice
- 600ml chicken or vegetable broth
- 300g chicken thighs, bone-in, skin-on
- 200g rabbit meat, cut into pieces (optional)
- 150g green beans, trimmed

- 1 red bell pepper, sliced
- 1 tomato, grated
- 1 onion, finely chopped
- 3 cloves garlic, minced
- 1/2 teaspoon saffron threads
- 1 teaspoon smoked paprika
- Olive oil
- Salt and pepper to taste

Instructions:

1. Use smoked paprika, salt, and pepper to season the chicken thighs.
2. In a big skillet or paella pan, heat the olive oil over medium-high heat. The chicken thighs should be browned on both sides. Remove them and set them aside.
3. If necessary, add extra olive oil to the same pan. If using, sauté the rabbit meat until it turns brown. Remove it and place it aside.
4. Add the onion and sauté it in the pan until tender. Add the garlic and cook until aromatic.
5. Add the grated tomato and heat, stirring, until it breaks down, a few minutes.
6. Add the rice to the pan and stir continuously for one to two minutes.
7. Pour the saffron threads and the remaining stock into the pan after dissolving them in a ladleful of warm broth. Heat through to a simmer.
8. Top the rice with the chicken thighs, red bell pepper, green beans, and rabbit meat.
9. Cook the rice for 15 to 20 minutes or until it is soft and the liquid has been absorbed. 10. Before serving, remove

the paella Valenciana from the stove and let it rest. Warm it up and top it with wedges of lemon.

Spanish Crumbly Bread Dish

Ingredients:

- 500g stale bread, cut into small cubes
- 100ml olive oil
- 4 cloves garlic, minced
- 2 dried chilli peppers, chopped (optional)
- 1 teaspoon smoked paprika
- Salt to taste
- 200g chorizo, sliced (optional)
- 200g bacon, diced (optional)
- 3 eggs, fried (optional)

Instructions:

1. Use smoked paprika, salt, and pepper to season the chicken thighs.
2. In a big skillet or paella pan, heat the olive oil over medium-high heat. The chicken thighs should be browned on both sides. Remove them and set them aside.
3. If necessary, add extra olive oil to the same pan. If using, sauté the rabbit meat until it turns brown. Remove it and place it aside.
4. Add the onion and sauté it in the pan until tender. Add the garlic and cook until aromatic.
5. Add the grated tomato and heat, stirring, until it breaks down, a few minutes.
6. Add the rice to the pan and stir continuously for one to two minutes.

7. Pour the saffron threads and the remaining stock into the pan after dissolving them in a ladleful of warm broth. Heat through to a simmer.
8. Top the rice with the chicken thighs, red bell pepper, green beans, and rabbit meat.
9. Cook the rice for 15 to 20 minutes or until it is soft and the liquid has been absorbed. 10. Before serving, remove the paella Valenciana from the stove and let it rest. Warm it up and top it with wedges of lemon.

Spanish Pumpkin Soup

Ingredients:

- 1 kg pumpkin, peeled and diced
- 1 onion, chopped
- 2 cloves garlic, minced
- 1 potato, peeled and diced
- 1 liter vegetable broth
- 100ml heavy cream
- Olive oil
- Salt and pepper to taste
- Pumpkin seeds and croutons for garnish (optional)

Instructions:

1. In a big pot over medium heat, warm the olive oil. Cook the minced garlic and onion until they become tender.
2. Add the diced potato and pumpkin to the pot and cook, stirring occasionally, for a few minutes.
3. Add the veggie broth and heat through. Simmer the vegetables for 20 to 25 minutes or until they are soft.

4. Puree the soup with an immersion blender until it's smooth. Or, put the soup in a blender and purée it until it's soft, then pour it back into the pot.
5. Add the heavy cream and taste-test the salt and pepper.
6. If preferred, top the hot pumpkin soup with croutons or pumpkin seeds. Savour this cosy and creamy Spanish soup!

CHAPTER - 18
CONTEMPORARY INTERPRETATIONS OF SPANISH BAKING

Modern culinary trends and advances are combined with traditional ingredients and techniques to create contemporary interpretations of Spanish baking. Spanish baking has a long history and has been inspired by many different cultures, such as Arabic, Jewish, and Roman. This has led to a wide variety of flavours and baking methods. Traditional Spanish bread and pastries have been reimagined in recent years by bakers and chefs, who have kept the spirit of the original recipes while adding fresh flavours, ingredients, and presentation techniques.

Here are some critical aspects of contemporary interpretations of Spanish baking:

Creative Flavors: While adhering to traditional recipes, modern Spanish bakers frequently play around with novel taste combinations and ingredients. To produce distinctive flavour profiles, they could add savoury components like chorizo or saffron, or even matcha, yuzu, and cardamom, to traditional pastries.

Health-Conscious Options: Many modern Spanish bakers are providing healthier options that include whole grains, natural sugars, and healthier fats in response to the increased demand for baked goods. These selections satisfy customers seeking tasty and healthful delights.

Artisanal Bread Making: Spain is not an exception to the global trend of artisanal bread making's comeback in popularity. To produce bread with intricate flavours and textures, modern bakers are concentrating on traditional methods of bread-making, such as sourdough fermentation and lengthy proofing periods.

Regional Influences: Modern bakers frequently take inspiration from the distinctive culinary traditions of Spain's many regions. Bakers use regional ingredients and methods in their creations, as seen in the creamy desserts of Catalonia, the almond-based sweets of Andalusia, and the rustic bread of Galicia.

Creative Presentation: Spanish bakers today place equal emphasis on presentation as they do on taste and texture, giving their creations a striking visual appeal. Artistic garnishes, vibrant glazes, and intricate pastry designs are employed to improve the entire eating experience.

Cross-Cultural Fusion: Instead of adhering to geographical boundaries, Spanish baking now welcomes influences from all around the world. Modern adaptations can create inventive and fascinating new dishes by fusing ingredients from various cuisines, such as American baking traditions, Asian taste profiles, or French pastry techniques.

Stress on High-Quality Ingredients: Spanish baking strongly emphasizes using high-quality, locally sourced ingredients, much like other modern culinary trends. Whether it's seasonal fruits, farm-fresh eggs, or organic flour, bakers give top priority to components that improve the flavour and calibre of their baked goods.

Modern Techniques: Modern equipment and techniques are employed by Spanish bakers today to increase consistency and streamline manufacturing processes while honouring ancient practices. This could involve using vacuum infusion, sous vide cooking, or precise temperature control.

Modern takes on Spanish baking combine creativity and tradition to create a colourful and lively culinary scene that never fails to enthral locals and tourists alike.

CONCLUSION

To sum up, the Spanish Baking Cookbook is a pleasant culinary adventure that offers a wide variety of recipes that encapsulate the essence of Spain's rich cultural legacy. Readers have been introduced to a wide range of savoury and sweet sweets through the pages of this cookbook, all of which are filled with the lively flavours and fragrances that characterize Spanish baking.

This cookbook offers a wide variety of dishes fit for any occasion, from the classic churros and flan to the less well-known treats like empanadas and pellets. It may be used for a big celebration or a quiet afternoon snack. Furthermore, the book's inclusion of historical anecdotes and cultural insights has enhanced both the culinary experience and readers' understanding of Spain's culinary heritage.

In addition, the clear directions and practical advice guarantee that bakers of all skill levels can successfully replicate these delicious treats in their kitchens. This cookbook gives readers the confidence and creativity to take on their baking endeavours, whether it's polishing the crust of an ensaimada or striking the perfect balance of sweetness in a tarta de Santiago.

The Spanish Baking Cookbook is really a celebration of Spanish culture, tradition, and the joy of baking rather than merely a compilation of recipes. It encourages readers to relish each taste along with the stories and memories that go along with the flavours of Spain. May this cookbook inspire years to come of culinary inquiry and admiration for the delectable pleasures of Spanish baking while the aroma of freshly baked goodies fills the air.

The End

Printed in Dunstable, United Kingdom